I AM ARMY 2

WE DON'T NEED PERMISSION

I AM ARMY 2

WE DON'T NEED PERMISSION

Edited by

Wallea Eaglehawk,
Michelle Bùi Hoàng &
M. Anastasia Kinderman

BULLETPROOF
Meanjin, Australia

ISBN 978-0-6453392-6-0

Cover by Jeremy Monroy, Purple Studio

First published in 2023

Bulletproof
Meanjin, Australia
www.bulletproof.revolutionaries.com.au

CONTENTS

Related Titles

From Bulletproof

I Am ARMY: It's Time to Begin edited by Wallea Eaglehawk and Courtney Lazore

Love Yourself: Essays on self-love, care and healing inspired by BTS edited by Wallea Eaglehawk and Keryn Ibrahim

BTS by ARMY: 2020 edited by Wallea Eaglehawk

From Revolutionaries

Idol Limerence: The Art of Loving BTS as Phenomena by Wallea Eaglehawk

From Moonrise

Through the darkness, I will love myself edited by Wallea Eaglehawk, Nikola Champlin and Padya Paramita

Contributors

Editors

Wallea Eaglehawk is an Australian-American author, poet and sociologist known best for her debut book *Idol Limerence*. She is the CEO of micro-publisher, Revolutionaries, and a full-time fangirl at The BTS Theorist. Find her on Twitter, Instagram, and TikTok @walleaeaglehawk, and on Instagram as @thebtstheorist.

Michelle Bùi Hoàng **(Phương Thảo Michelle Bùi Hoàng)** is a healthcare consultant, eclectic artist and former radiation therapist. She is a proud advocate for Asian representation, mental health and BTS. Outside of her professional life, Michelle is a dog mum to Sir Winston, ice cream connoisseur and a reading aficionado. Find her on Instagram @moshimish.

M. Anastasia Kinderman has enjoyed copy editing for Revolutionaries and editing her first book with both Wallea and Michelle. In her spare time she enjoys visiting art galleries and historical locations. She also likes turtles and, of course, the colour purple. Find her on Instagram @mijaneith.

Essayists

Lyndon Zass is a researcher by day, an eternal student by night, a full-time ARMY, and an aspiring content creator in between from Cape Town, South Africa. As a genetics and bioinformatics scholar, he spends most of his time in front of a computer. His true passions and pleasures, however, are travelling and working with new people from across Africa and the world, engaging in arts and culture, and advocating for social justice. You can find him on Twitter @lj_zass and Instagram @dreamcatcher.92.

Ashley Sue Bullers is a soul explorer and artist living in the Bangtan Vortex. Walking through the doors into her own Chapter Two, Ashley continues her fight to be 'still life', in training to become living proof of the *Permission* and *Love Yourself* era messages. She created the Bangtan Soul community and Epiphanatics podcast, where she and ARMY explore the intersection of midlife, mental health, and BTS. Besides BTS, Ashley Sue swoons wildly over love, her family, coffee, documentaries, and typeface. Find her on YouTube @AshleySueBangtanSoul and on Instagram and Twitter @ashleysue.

Paola Cristina Rivera Santos is an aspiring author and an English graduate from Puerto Rico. She started writing creatively from a young age and dreams of publishing novels and poetry collections. Now residing in New York City, she spends her free time travelling, writing, and exploring. In addition to liking BTS, she is also interested in popular culture studies and photography. You can find her ARMY account on Instagram @moonkives.

Gardênia Pereira is a Brazilian psychologist, neuropsychologist, and writer. She researches fandom behaviour and the influence of music, promoting discussions on mental health. She can be found on Instagram @gardeniapereiira @psigardenia and Medium @gardeniapereira.

Bianca Cuatico is an auxiliar de conversación (language assistant) based in Madrid, Spain and is helping kids improve their English communication skills. Until recently, she lived her whole life in the Philippines and was a recruitment supervisor for a multinational business process outsourcing company doing volume hiring. Her interests are in true crime docu-series, reading, skincare, learning about different cultures and mythologies, and of course, BTS. She is also a supporter of animal welfare and wildlife conservation organisations. You can find her on Instagram @biancacuatico.

Emily Dunham is a writer, poet, ARMY, and animal advocate. She holds a B.S. in animal behaviour with minors in biology and creative writing. She is currently a canine behaviour team member at a city animal shelter and enjoys creating training plans and marketing strategies for the dogs prior to adoption. She has been writing since childhood and her poetry has been published on Rising Phoenix Review. Besides BTS, her interests include reading, weightlifting, music, and skincare. You can find her on TikTok @emviolet7.

Martyna Kučinskaitė is a pianist, poet and writer from Lithuania. She is currently tutoring students Lithuanian as well as teaching music. Her piano performances can be found on

YouTube @martynakucinskaite, and her article *Transformations of Identity in the Newest Prose by Lithuanian Women* can be found in OIKOS. Martyna enjoys composing music, learning new languages, travelling, cooking, giving gifts to dear people, constantly consuming art and expressing herself in a variety of art forms. Soon she is planning to publish her first poetry collection as well as release more music. Find her on Instagram @sauletos_pievos.

Ran Rice is an academic and writer from Minneapolis, Minnesota. Having recently graduated from University of Minnesota his studies were primarily focused in psychology and gender and queer Studies. Beyond BTS and K-pop, he is passionate about healthcare for all and advocates for trans rights within healthcare systems and social policy. You can find him on Twitter @chickenbitz_ and Instagram @chickenbitz_ and @chcknbtz.

We don't need permission (to be ARMY)

Wallea Eaglehawk

2023 DOESN'T FEEL like it has yet begun despite it being January 30. I'm sitting in a library on a balmy summer day. It's hot and sticky, the aircon barely feels cold. I can see families outside enjoying the sunshine. By all means, this experience is quintessentially Australian, though I haven't seen a kangaroo in quite some time.

Across the road is a cafe I have frequented for the better part of four years. I distinctly remember sitting there when first selecting essays for this book. I would perch on a stool in an area at the back of the cafe and watch people come and go. I always thought it was strange that I was sitting there reading work from ARMY from all around the world while life carried on around me. No one coming and going knew what I was doing, no one particularly cared. I think two of the baristas and the owner knew the nature of my work because they kept up with my vlogs. But to them, this was just another day in the life of me, a local writer-slash-publisher. Nothing extraordinary. For me, however, it was a special day and an important time. I was heralding a new group of essayists that, I hoped, would soon convey the ARMY experience to the world.

What I didn't know then, was that this would soon become the longest anthology project I had ever taken on. Despite my best intentions and an enthusiasm to exceed expectations, it didn't quite get off the ground. I write to you today one year past the original slated publication date. I was originally going to write about how it had been a long time between books–*I Am ARMY: It's time to begin* came out September 2020–and that so much had transpired in the world, with BTS and within the fandom. Now, it truly has been a long time. The video of RM in the studio saying "it's been a year" comes to mind, "it's been a motherfucking year."[1] And isn't that the truth.

I digress.

So there I was, reading essays while the world moved on around me. The people I saw were very likely not aware of who BTS were, and the chances were slim that they were ARMY. A vast juxtaposition to the world I frequented online where every piece of content I saw–voluntarily or not–was about BTS. Every conversation revolved around them. Every disagreement I bore witness to in comment sections was about them. Even when I was in spaces that were typically non-BTS dominated, they'd somehow appear. In my internal world and the vast internet scape, they remained omnipresent. Increasingly so as the pandemic wore on.

I'm bringing up this juxtaposition because it plays a part in how I put together books for Bulletproof. Though it's an imprint that is dedicated to publishing books about BTS and ARMY, its tagline is that it publishes books for discerning fans *and* curious onlookers alike. I am not interested in publishing books for ARMY and ARMY alone for I fear that will create an echo chamber. My interest not only lies in locating, documenting, disseminating and celebrating the diverse voice of ARMY. It also lies in providing means for scholars and the general public to get an authentic understanding of what it means to be ARMY, and the impact of BTS. A living record of the life of ARMY, if you like. Albeit it 10 at a time. But it's a start, it's a glimpse, it's real and honest and raw. It's not sugar coated, though it can be sweet. It's life through the lens and experience of fandom. From both the inside and the periphery.

My role as editor is to make decisions that shape the book into a bridge from the essayists to not only other ARMY, but to whoever might take an interest. That is why the juxtaposition is often–though I believe to be subconsciously–intentionally sought. I must keep one foot in the world of BTS and ARMY and the other in my quintessential Australian experience.

In my writing, I often see myself as a channel for the collective. I observe ARMY, I observe the world, I observe myself and I live straddling many juxtapositions and paradoxes and complexities. I synthesise it all through my creative and scholarly process and turn it into a poem, an essay, a chapter or a book. The end result is what I hope is something that is painfully specific but universally understood.

In my editing of anthologies, I am the curator. I put out a request for submissions and I then must work with the material I receive. I must take great care in reading and understanding what has been sent to me; for these are stories that are deeply personal and meaningful to each writer. I must determine which essays are the right fit for the book, and I must determine which essays are worth the gamble. The problem, of course, is that each submission is perfect just the way it is. It is representative of that unique ARMY's journey. It's very much an artefact. As an ARMY and as a writer, I empathise with every essayist who doesn't make it. But as a curator, an editor, a publisher, I have to think about how best to represent the fandom to the world. What stories do I want to share? What themes have arisen? Are the essays saying the same thing as the previous collection? These are just some of the thoughts that bounce around not only during the selection process, but the development of the essays, too.

For this book, I was joined by my co-editors Michelle and M who not only worked hard on selecting and developing the essays alongside the essayists, but contributed their own, too. Just like me, Michelle and M are avid ARMY, which is, of course, how we came to know one another. I am incredibly grateful to have shared this project with them, as it's even more meaningful when shared with friends and ARMY.

Similar to my writing, the result of these anthologies is what I hope to be a series of books that are painfully specific–the ARMY experience–and universally understood–what it means to be human. What it means to love. What it means to grieve. What it means to persist. What it means to want more and be more. What it means to *be*, together.

This is the fourth anthology on BTS and ARMY that I have put together, and the fourth time I feel the need to introduce BTS to you. Funny, considering the vast majority of eyes perceiving these words will already know who they are. But if, by chance, you are new to these acronyms, and in turn, the BTSverse and fandom as a whole, this might be useful.

BTS, short for 방탄소년단, Bangtan Sonyeondan—in English, Bulletproof Boy Scouts—are a seven-member group from Seoul,

South Korea. The members are 김남준, Kim Namjoon, *RM*; 김석진, Kim Seokjin, *Jin*; 민윤기, Min Yoongi, *Suga*; 정호석, Jung Hoseok, *j-hope*; 박지민, Park Jimin, *Jimin*; 김태형, Kim Taehyung, *V*; and, 전정국, Jeon Jungkook; *Jung Kook*.

ARMY, an acronym for Adorable Representative M.C. for Youth, is the name given by BTS to their fanbase. In trying to define ARMY back in 2020 I wrote that "it can be difficult to summarise ARMY in so few words; they are a true cross-section of the world. Or, perhaps it would be better to describe them as a microcosm of humankind—a *mikrokosmos* if you like."[2] This still rings true, though it continues to frustrate me that I cannot succinctly communicate the fandom in a way that does them justice. That is where this book comes in handy, though. Instead of me telling you who ARMY are, it's better if they do it themselves.

I still believe that there's a great need for sharing ARMY stories within fandom and further afield. Firstly, to create a living document of the here and now. One that celebrates the diverse experiences of fandom and of being human. And through this, creating something that gives back to the community and shows the innate value of personal stories, no matter how big or small. This is a book by ARMY for ARMY, after all.

Secondly, I believe the world still wants to know what exactly makes BTS so good. For people on the outside looking in, they see a juggernaut. But BTS hasn't always been that way. To listen to the general narrative about the group and their fandom is to hear a lot of stereotypes and judgements. BTS are often dismissed as inferior musicians, ARMY are often reduced to hysterical fangirls. Yet despite a lack of recognition for the phenomenon of both BTS and ARMY, they continue to go from strength to strength. This book is one of many pieces of work that exists to show the un-media tainted truth. A truth rooted in the mundane, human existence. BTS are BTS because of ARMY, and there's much to be learned from reading, watching and listening to fandom stories. To understand ARMY, in a sense, is to understand BTS. For the two are a mirror of one another–just as ARMY serve as a microcosm of human kind, BTS serve as a microcosm of ARMY.

I Am ARMY is a study of fandom, of identity, and the potential of mass social power in the name of self-love. For as long as fandoms are devalued, there will be a need for books such as this. A greater understanding and appreciation is needed, for I truly believe that to know ARMY, to see them and hold space for all their complexities, is to know the world. Know the micro to know the macro. And right now, there are people out there who are violently criticising and rejecting the fan, the inner child, the untamed desire in us all.

This is where this book's subtitle of *we don't need permission* comes from. It firstly draws inspiration from BTS' song *Permission to Dance* with the lyric "we don't need permission to dance",[3] and from the essays within the book. And, secondly, it gives space for a wide range of ARMY experiences. When thinking of a fandom, it's easy to assume that there are rules and conditions for entry. Perhaps you need to know every single song and every single lyric of BTS', perhaps you need to own all their merchandise. Perhaps, perhaps, perhaps. When thinking of a fandom, it's easy to assume that each member is the same. Media representations of fans would have us think of a young, hysterical woman who will soon grow out of her foolish ways. But of course, this is simply not true. There are no hard rules for being an ARMY, except one: Love BTS. And, most importantly, there is no particular demographic that defines the fandom. Though there are certain demographics that are larger or more prominent than others, ARMY is more diverse, fluid, and ever-changing. ARMY is *more*. And above all else, we don't need permission.

We don't need permission to be ARMY. We don't need permission to find joy with BTS. We don't need permission to express our desires, hopes and dreams. We don't need permission to work together to show our love for music, for art, for one another. We don't need permission to explore and express who we are. We don't need permission to live life on our own terms. And, if BTS have taught us anything, we definitely don't need permission to love ourselves, even in our darkest hour, even on our darkest of days.

Within these pages you will find experiences ranging from the mundane of daily life to the extremes of sorrow, from small moments of joy to existential philosophising on identity. There are ten stories of how BTS has changed, shaped, inspired, disrupted and saved lives of ARMY from around the world. Ten different experiences of the same phenomenon. Ten different ways ARMY have not sought permission to be themselves, oftentimes the journey being just that–one of discovering, through BTS, that we do not need permission at all.

There must be a reason that this book took so long to complete. I hope the reason is that it came out at the right time to find you when you needed it most. I trust that these essays will resonate and provide a source of inspiration and comfort to whoever is in need. I would be remiss if I didn't extend my heartfelt thanks to my co-editors Michelle and M, and to the essayists Lyndon, Ashley Sue, Paola, Gardênia, Bianca, Emily, Martyna, and Ran. None of this would be possible without you, and I'm beyond thrilled to be sharing your stories with the world.

To you, whose eyes are currently reading my words, thank you for picking up this book. If this is your first time with us, welcome. If you've been reading these collections over the years, it's good to have you back. Whether you are ARMY, doing some research or a genuinely curious onlooker, I hope you find what you're looking for here.

If you are to take anything away from this book may it be that you don't need permission to be you, ARMY or not. And that no matter where you are on your journey, you are not alone. We are all here figuring this life out, learning, growing, doing and being together. I truly wouldn't have it any other way.

References

1 BANGTANTV. (2014). *[EPISODE] BTS (방탄소년단) 1st anniversary - so 4 more* [Video]. https://www.youtube.com/watch?v=LchUwgPashw

2 Eaglehawk, W. (2020). Enter the magic shop: Introducing I am ARMY. In W. Eaglehawk & C. Lazore (Eds.), *I am ARMY: It's time to begin*. Bulletproof.

3 BTS. (2021). *Permission to dance* [Song]. Big Hit Entertainment.

Journey to my heart

Lyndon Zass

On

WE LIVE IN a world that teaches us from a young age that we are unworthy of love and happiness. Before we even learn how to write and read properly, we are introduced–both explicitly and implicitly–to a standard of living we should aspire towards. While it may vary between regions, the standard usually includes some form of a white picket fence, a traditional nuclear family, a luxurious lifestyle, conventionally attractive looks, and an unwavering happy and selfless demeanour. For most, if not all, of us, this standard is impossible to achieve. Yet anything less is considered a failure. So, we fail... and fail... and fail yet again. We keep on failing, and with each failure, we have yet another reason to dislike ourselves. Whether it's something about how we look, how we act or what we do, somehow, we always fall short. As our minds and bodies grow, so does our mental checklist–things we need to fix in order to unlock the door to happiness. The never-ending journey to unattainable happiness is a trap, one that we slip into as unconsciously as we do a dream, night after night, time and time again. But what if happiness is not something we need to achieve, to work towards, or to unlock?

Twenty-one years after I was born, a seven-member boy band called BTS debuted, and although I would only discover them seven years later, they would turn out to be the greatest discovery I could ever make. This is the story of how BTS challenged me with this very question on happiness, and by doing so, journeyed into my heart and changed my life forever. An unexpected, irrevocable, and inexplicable journey. Not towards external achievement, but rather internal fulfilment. With me as their stupendously naïve but eternally grateful passenger.

Butterfly

In the recently released *Knives Out* instalment, *Glass Onion*, the movie spotlights the similarly named metaphor; the concept of something being both multi-layered and transparent at the same time, both complex and simple.[1] In the very same way, the journey I describe here may initially seem a complex one, but as I peel back the layers of my life, it becomes extremely apparent that BTS' journey into my soul was a foregone conclusion from the jump.

I was born one month before Jin, about halfway across the world, in South Africa. This was, in fact, two years before the country achieved true democracy and ended the apartheid regime.[2] Therefore, most of my formative years were marked by a period of national transformation.

South Africa is often referred to as a rainbow nation, due to its cultural diversity. But for much of my childhood, this remained a curious description. I grew up in a racially and culturally homogenous community, and engagements with the country's trademark diversity were limited to glances in stores and the worlds unfolding on my TV screen. Despite these barriers, however, I developed a unique fascination with culture and diversity; I was always glued to the TV, curious about where and how people who did not look like me lived. In retrospect, I'm sure some of this fascination was driven by a feeling of estrangement. Although I could not describe or understand it at the time, I knew that I was somehow different and did not fit into my surroundings.

Growing up as a young South African coloured[3] boy and only child, this feeling of estrangement became a constant companion, and the first indicator that I would not be able to unlock the lauded standard of happiness. Despite having a naturally whacky and outgoing personality, I started building a wall in preparation for defence. Within my inner circle I was quirky, passionate, flamboyant and sometimes loud, while on the outside I was introverted, shy, reserved and quiet. In this way, an interesting juxtaposition formed within me, an eternal optimist, fascinated by the world at large, but terrified of it as well, paralysed and mute at the thought of venturing outside my comfort zone. I often see a similar juxtaposition among BTS in their older videos. Their playful nature is infectious and naïve ambition inspiring, but they're also burdened with external and self-imposed expectations beyond compare, and riddled with a fear of exhibiting their true selves. Many of my childhood memories are filled with the same type of joy, fear, and burden of expectation. Letting go of that burden is something that I would struggle with for many years to come.

Whalien 52

When I started digging into BTS' discography, I was struck by the way they could balance the ugly and beautiful so well within their work, either through their lyrics on tracks such as *Blooming Youth*, vocals on *House of Cards*, or visuals in *I Need You*. It made me reflect on my life from a different perspective. Typically, embarrassing moments where my walls were accidentally lowered and I was revealed as an imposter are carved into my mind. While happier moments easily fade with time. This is why *The Most Beautiful Moment in Life* trilogy remains my personal favourite amongst BTS' stellar discography. Although geared to the youth, the trilogy's message can be applied throughout life, and remains a strong source of strength and support for me to this day, as I bridge the age of 30.

Adolescence is typically marked by a loss of innocence,[4] and this was true for my experience as well. My teenage years were dreadful, to say the least, marked by a loss of self and battle scars which I still deal with today.

The beginning of the end started when my family relocated, and I was ripped from the comfort zone I was so accustomed to. Suddenly I was forced to face new surroundings, new people, new dynamics and new social situations; I was not at all prepared. Now, more than ever before, I needed my wall of defence to be higher and sturdier. Like a turtle in danger, I retracted into my shell for protection. I was more reserved than ever and went by without a friend for over two whole years. My self-esteem was crushed, and my growth was stunted. When I wasn't busy dreaming of living in a fantasy world, my internal discussion was at war, desperately searching for resolution. The introspection wasn't without value, as I started to unpack my unfortunate situation and the growing list of insecurities preventing me from happiness.

In my new school, I suddenly found myself living in a more accurate representation of the South African rainbow nation. Because of my previous environment, I had never experienced racial discrimination, but now I suddenly realised how the colour of my skin influenced how others perceived me. Though not intentional, I felt a sense of 'othering' when forced into social situations and expected to get along with people who looked like me. To make matters worse, I was finally able to describe the differences I felt as a child–I was queer. The wall of defence was no longer just that, it was a closet as well. A place where I could suppress everything that didn't adhere to the standard of happiness I was taught, to keep the hope of achieving that standard alive. All while being constantly afraid to say or do the wrong thing, and to draw any type of attention, positive or negative. No longer was I in my comfort zone, and, at times, my paralysis and mutism became alarmingly literal.

I often wonder what my life would've been like if I had BTS around at the time. Their music speaks to all the struggles I was facing. The *Love Yourself* trilogy illustrates the desire to be loved and supported, either by yourself, your partner, your friends or family, as well as the fear that you may either lose or never have that love at all. Songs like *You Never Walk Alone* make the painful moments a little less painful, and the lonely moments a lot less lonely. I get chills every time I listen to it. Knowing that other people are enduring the same struggles I did would've helped a ton. The social labels thrust upon me felt like a steel cross I had no choice but to bear. The more I tried to hide them, the more obvious they would become, like gigantic scarlet letters. My optimism had faded, and so had my wanderlust. The diversity I had previously been so fascinated with suddenly became a source of great terror. I felt ashamed on most days and became my own biggest enemy. I had no dreams or ambition of my own, I only cared about adhering to a standard I could never achieve.

Moving On

As I grew older, I started to care less; one of the benefits that come with age. As if injected by morphine, things started to feel less intense, urgent and exaggerated. Despite this transition, however, I had not resolved any of my trauma. My shadow companions lingered, constantly reminding me of my inadequacy and ineptitude.

University offered me a rare opportunity to reinvent myself, be everything I couldn't be in high school. I completely ignored this chance and, instead, opted for a quick fix. I recreated the comfort zone of my childhood, a comfortable community of shared culture and race, void of diversity. This seemed to work. Suddenly I had friends again, people who I could laugh and have fun with. However, the comfort was fleeting. Unlike the naïve child of the past, I had become all too aware of my lack of authenticity, and it prevented me from building stable and sustainable relationships. Friendships are built on trust, shared experiences, ambitions, fears and struggles, but I had no such experiences to share. I had barely lived at all. I was too afraid, trapped in a closet that was bursting at the seams. The cycle seemed to be on repeat, and I kept finding myself back at step one, all alone and with no solution in sight.

A reversal of fortune came upon me, not by any act of my own, but by some divine intervention out of my control. I found myself in a new environment yet again and started the search for my next comfort zone. This time, however, due to circumstances of time, place and chance, I found myself unintentionally broadening and diversifying my social circle. I started surrounding myself with confident individuals who possessed progressive voices, unique perspectives, and diverse backgrounds. I could finally embrace the diversity I had grown to fear, and I was inspired. Slowly but surely, I started accepting the labels that I once believed prevented my happiness. They inspired me to embrace my culture, take pride in my African roots, to embrace my culture, and live by a strong set of guiding principles that were my own, no matter how strange and unique they may be.

This reminds me of when RM in his United Nations speech said "We have learned to love ourselves, so now I urge you to "speak yourself.""[5] Speaking yourself doesn't always mean speaking with ambition, eloquence, and confidence, I learned. Being in touch with your emotions, sharing your feelings and your vulnerability is equally empowering, if not more, as exemplified by BTS throughout their career. With these new lessons in mind, I became empowered with the knowledge that I had found a community of love and trust, where I could share my dreams, desires, fears and struggles. I lowered the wall of defence and unlocked the closet I had been hiding in. I was met with nothing but overwhelming support and a rush of serotonin when I came out. The labels that had dragged me down for so many years before became flags which I raised high in the sky with pride. A weight had been lifted off my shoulders and I had learned to love myself. Right?

I had confidently progressed into the next stage of my life, I settled into work, and lived a generally happy and enjoyable existence. However, something still felt off, a hint of cynicism remained. Embracing your labels, I've come to find out, is only half the journey.

Just One Day

I still remember the first day I properly discovered BTS very clearly. It was a gloomy September day, an unusual start to spring, which seemed to match the unpredictable and sombre turn the COVID-19 ridden year had taken. I felt overworked, underpaid, and worn out. I had just come off from a laboured August month and I was in desperate need for a pick me up.

I was procrastinating and somehow found myself watching performances from the 2020 MTV Video Music Awards which had just aired a few days earlier. I only intended to watch Doja Cat and Ariana Grande, but then I spotted the BTS performance in the corner of my eye.

My previous encounters with K-pop had been brief and largely uneventful, limited to a couple of Twice, Loona and KARD tracks. Though I loved the whimsical nature of the music and the slick production as well, I wasn't inspired to dig any deeper. Interestingly, I later remembered that this *Spring Day* wouldn't be my first encounter with BTS either, I had briefly listened to *DNA* once before, but since I didn't understand the language, I dismissed it and moved on. This time, however, I was intrigued, I had just come upon a TikTok which included *Dynamite*. I loved the song on first listen and downloaded it immediately. The VMAs would be my first opportunity to see the song performed live and, though I had absolutely no expectations heading into the performance, I was keen to see whether the band could deliver on the promise of the catchy pop track. What happened next could only be described in one way–I was struck by lightning! I was mesmerised, impressed, charmed, in love, joyful and teary-eyed all at the same time. It was, unlike anything I've experienced before, and I fell faster than a comet. It felt like I had just encountered seven angels, and then they added fireworks! I was sold and needed to know more!

The next steps were obvious, I needed to watch the *Dynamite* music video, and then a couple of reaction videos to the music video as well. Surely this was not normal behaviour, to be so impressed and intrigued by a musical act so quickly? I spent the better part of the rest of the day watching and re-watching the music video, and reaction videos to it. Without realising it, I had buckled up and set forth on a journey of no return. I needed to know, hear, and see more. Like Jung Kook losing a physical challenge, BTS' emergence into my life was completely unexpected, blasting through my rib cage and straight to my heart on day one. *Serendipity*.

I started diving into their music almost immediately, first listening to their single releases and watching a few more music videos. Naturally, I was drawn to the *Love Yourself* trilogy due to my past. I became more and more intrigued by the day, but I think I truly became an ARMY when I listened to my first full-length BTS album, *BE*. Leading up to its release, I had already felt an anticipation for the album unlike anything I've felt before. *BE* was released and BTS delivered on every ounce of expectation that I had formed, capturing my lockdown experiences so perfectly on the eight-track album, and with such variety to top it off. Released only two months after I discovered BTS, it felt silly to be so invested in the music and success of a band I had barely been familiar with a few weeks before. Yet there I was, eagerly participating in trying to get *Life Goes On* to break a YouTube record, waiting in suspense to see if it could debut at number one on the Billboard Hot 100. There was no turning back, and I needed to know how and why? What was so special about these seven boys? It seemed like their destination was set, the GPS was locked, and they were driving forward at full speed. I never stood a chance.

Answer: Love Myself

After discovering BTS, the succeeding few months feel like a blur, one I would happily relive given the choice. Since then, a day does not go by without me listening to at least one BTS-related song or engaging with some type of BTS content. Falling into the BTS rabbit hole truly feels like entering a fantasy world in which a beautiful discovery is made every other day. Two years later, and I still come upon content that I haven't seen before. Everything about the band appeals to me. I can connect to every story portrayed by their lyrics. I love the genre blending in their music, their style is captivating, their 'charisma, uniqueness, nerve, and talent'[6] is truly unmatched! Despite living worlds apart, I am struck by how relatable their journey, struggles and personalities are.

"Maybe I made a mistake yesterday, but yesterday's me is still me. I am who I am today, with all my faults. Tomorrow I might be a tiny bit wiser, and that's me, too. These faults and mistakes are what I am, making up the brightest stars in the constellation of my life. I have come to love myself for who I was, who I am, and who I hope to become."[5] On the surface, the *Love Yourself/Love Myself* concept may seem simple and cliché, but because we live in a world that constantly tells us we are not worthy, the practice of self-love is actually much more difficult. I had previously thought I had reached the point of fully loving myself, but the above quote from RM made me realise I did not fully grasp the entire concept. Though I wasn't starting completely from scratch, I still had a long way to go. Due to the difficult times I had in high school, I had been too hyper-focused on loving those parts of myself which I felt prevented me from having a much more enjoyable adolescence. Thus far, my *Love Myself* journey was limited to loving the social labels I had previously been taught to hate, but that's only half the journey.

I now realise there are many other parts of my being that also need to be embraced and voiced, I'm much more than just the social labels I tried to suppress in the past. BTS helped me to re-identify with my inner being, pick up the parts of myself that I had previously discarded during my struggles and efforts to be accepted. After discovering BTS, I have finally learned to truly speak myself. I am a proud South African coloured and

African citizen! I am an out and proud queer man! But I am also much, much more! I am a proud ARMY! I am intelligent and thoughtful. I am passionate and optimistic. I love wearing jewellery and dancing to the beat of my own drum. I love playing and watching tennis. I love travelling and immersing myself into different cultures, talking to people all over the world, and learning from their experiences. With this enriched life that BTS has provided me, I can't wait to venture on a pilgrimage to Seoul, South Korea, one day.

A few years later, and I've only recently been able to put in words how BTS has sparked such a connection in me, how they have managed to journey to the centre of my heart. The answer is simple... They didn't embark on the journey alone, they took me by the hand, and allowed me to join. Because of BTS, I have learned so much about myself, I feel as though I've regained qualities I had lost prior. I have upgraded to a better version of myself, I am more socially conscious, empathetic, philanthropic, and happy.

Yet to Come (The Most Beautiful Moment)

I recently came upon a video by Ashley Sue, a YouTuber and fellow ARMY, in which she mentions that middle-aged people usually start grieving the life they wanted to live and expected of themselves when they were younger,[7] and although I just turned 30, the statement was meaningful and alluded to some emotions I had already started to feel in my own life. As a child, teenager and young adult, I had spent too much of my time chasing dreams that weren't mine. Till recently, I never gave my inner child an opportunity to chase their own dream. I was too afraid, as j-hope said in a recent Vanity Fair quiz, the future is scary.[8] But I'm not afraid anymore. During promotion for *The Most Beautiful Moment in Life,* RM says, "Happiness is not something that you have to achieve, you can still feel happy during the process of achieving something."[9] These are words I live by today.

I've recently watched BTS' entire journey from the beginning through *The Rise of BANGTAN* series on YouTube.[10] Their journey alone is not what inspires me the most about them, but the character with which they have taken on their setbacks and challenges. They've inspired me to find my happiness, and grab my opportunities, even at a much older age. I move forward with the certainty that I will have setbacks and face challenges, but also with the assurance that I will have a constant source of support in BTS. My life motto today is another RM quote from VLive, "Tomorrow, let's be less lazy and more hard working, and become a person who loves himself."[11] BTS have taught me to pursuit my dreams and to repurpose them, because of them, I built up the confidence and courage to publish my first article[12] and submit my story to this book, But above all, BTS have taught me how to be happy, they've truly made the last years the most beautiful moment of my life!

To RM, Jin, Suga, j-hope, Jimin, V and Jung Kook, I'm not sure if you'll ever read what I have put down on paper here, but even if you read just a small section, I want you to know I am eternally grateful for the light you have introduced into my life. 'Imilingo' is a local South African word in the native language Xhosa, used to describe magic, which is what I now have because of you. I will work hard to hold onto that, to never dim that light again. Hwaiting!

References

[1] Johnson, R. (Director, Producer), & Bergman, R (Producer). (2022) Glass Onion: A Knives Out Mystery. T-Street Productions.

[2] Little, B. (2020). *Key Steps That Led to End of Apartheid*. History.com

[3] Adhikari, M. (2009). *Burdened By Race: Coloured Identities in Southern Africa*. UCT Press.

[4] Jones, B. (2019). *The Loss of Childhood Innocence*. Scienceleadership.org.

[5] BTS. (2018) *UN General Assembly Speech*. UNICEF. https://www.unicef.org/press-releases/we-have-learned-love-ourselves-so-now-i-urge-you-speak-yourself

[6] RuPaul. (2017). Charisma, Uniqueness, Nerve & Talent [Song]. On *American*. RuCo, Inc.

[7] Ashley Sue. (2021, Sept 10). *BTS Rise of Bangtan 9 reaction : It IS The Most Beautiful Moment in Life | 방탄소년단* [Video]. Youtube. https://www.youtube.com/watch?v=rt1khdd6zOI&ab_channel=AshleySue

[8] Vanity Fair. (2021, Aug 18). *How Well Does BTS Know Each Other? | BTS Game Show | Vanity Fair* [Video]. Youtube. https://www.youtube.com/watch?v=6jflOa_zgRc&t=18s&ab_channel=VanityFair

[9] BTS. (2015) *The Most Beautiful Moment in Life On Stage Tour* in Seoul. Big Hit Entertainment. 'In' esmeel. (2018). 8 times BTS's RM shared valuable pieces of wisdom. Soompi. https://www.soompi.com/article/1258945wpp/8-times-btss-rm-shared-

valuable-pieces-wisdom#:~:text=%E2%80%9CHappiness%20is%

[10] TheRiseOfBangtanOfficial. (2021, Jan 2). *THE RISE OF BANGTAN - Chapter 1: We Are Bulletproof* [Video]. Youtube. https://www.youtube.com/watch?v=QxAmkAwIEeY&t=13s&ab_channel=TheRiseOfBangtanOfficial

[11] TheRiseOfBangtanOfficial. (2021, Jan 2). *THE RISE OF BANGTAN - Chapter 16: My Time* [Video]. YouTube. https://www.youtube.com/watch?v=QxAmkAwIEeY&t=13s&ab_channel=TheRiseOfBangtanOfficial

[12] Zass, L. (2021). *The bubbly rise and appeal of K-pop.* Thought Leader. https://thoughtleader.co.za/the-bubbly-rise-and-appeal-of-k-pop/

Permission

Ashley Sue Bullers

I HAD SPENT 16 months planning how to end my life. I knew it was 'the' day when I sobbed uncontrollably while watching my two-year-old and three-year-old ride their bicycles for the first time. All I could think was, 'If I'm not happy in this perfect moment, I can't be saved'. Never could I dream that seven men whose names I did not know, in a language I did not understand, would keep me breathing that same day. Their voices became my heartbeat as they took me into an eight-hour intervention. I had no concept that in those hours a boy band could awaken within me a love, curiosity, and hope that I thought already died.

Before BTS found me, my life outwardly appeared great. Twenty years with my high school sweetheart, and after many years we now had two healthy children. Yet I had become weathered over the years. We blamed the infertility, my father's suicide, adoption scammers, and years of immovable job monotony for the disappearance of my sparkle. My marriage, once home to what I thought was the world's greatest love story, had become quiet and hard. We never really shared many interests, but we loved each other and were best friends. A decade of stress had eroded our openness, though, and in a constant attempt to avoid bothering each other, we lost our closeness also.

I usually blamed only myself for how hard our relationship had become. I hated myself. As a Christian with a privileged life and lovely family, who was I to feel so much anxiety and anger? I constantly wondered, 'What's wrong with me?' I had asked, to the point of begging sometimes, my husband for different things over the years. Let's consider moving, maybe closer to family; stop invalidating things I do; hold my hand more and kiss me deeply... and on and on and on. The same answers always came, becoming an endless echo in my head: Voices telling me I'm ungrateful. I'm too clingy. I'm too needy. I dream too much. It's not the right time.

Every time I heard those words, shame seared me. I apologised yet again for making things hard on us. I would remind myself that my family just shows their love through service, like keeping the cars running and doing home renovations together. Shame, telling me, 'I am the only one causing problems here, asking for so much. I am ruining their happiness by wanting more. I'm making them feel they aren't enough.' These echoes in my head grew louder each year. 'I am too emotional. I want too much. I need to grow up. Why do I need someone to say they love me?' The more I tried to appreciate love as service transactions, the angrier I became. I felt like I was being destroyed from the inside out, eventually giving in to planning my own destruction.

One day I had become too scared of myself, that I begged my husband for help in a true act of desperation. I felt I was gasping my last breaths, begging for resuscitation.

That was November 2019. Becoming 'Mama' had somehow created unprecedented loneliness, both in our marriage and within myself. We were 100 miles away from any family or friends, and emotionally miles away from each other with the distance only growing. I admitted in choking sobs to my husband, *my person*, that I was a few months into planning my suicide. I told him I needed to go to a mental health facility and had looked some up. He hugged me tightly... and within a few hours, we resumed the day like nothing had happened. The next day, I was sat down and told to find another therapist, to maybe go for more walks, and maybe wear more makeup, to feel better. I was told sternly, factually, what my assignment was. And the conversation was over.

I hadn't known how distant my marriage had grown until then. I shared the unthinkable, and I realised the person I trusted most in the world had zero idea how to be *with* me in this life. I felt so alone and had for so long, I wondered if I was human at all. I spent the next weeks wondering if God might create some of us to be soulless entities in human form, to help real humans discover true happiness with each other. In this swirl of loneliness the holidays vanished, I turned 40 on New Year's Day, and 2020 began.

As I fumbled into a new year, COVID-19 soon took the world hostage. Ahmaud Arbery and George Floyd's murders rocked America. The world was in disarray. Yet with no family nearby and my husband as an essential worker, my daily life hadn't changed at all. Each day was as lonely as the approximately 700+ days before. Or was it 7000+ days? My home was a bubble filled with emotional distance. I cried constantly, without any clarity about what was actually wrong. The more I tried to talk with my family about it, the more I was told things like 'we are meant to suffer in this life' or that I was being selfish. I felt desperate to escape myself — until I found the world of YouTube, where commentary channels became companionship, stimulation, and escape.

Months rolled on, and I felt connected to no one and nothing. I hungered to free my husband and children of a life tethered to me and my undefinable brokenness. Honestly, I mostly was desperate to stop hurting, and I could only think of one way to stop. I myself had become the echo in an empty cave, repeatedly asking for help but not being heard. 'Survive until I die' had become my mantra while I kept searching for any glimmer of hope that life could feel better.

BTS finds you

In October 2020, as I scrolled my YouTube feed, YouTube insisted I watch one particular video. For days, a shiny thumbnail kept appearing, featuring a car full of radiant men with James Corden. I eventually gave in and found myself swimming in 15 minutes of pure, goofy magic. YouTube rewarded me by immediately recommending the happiest song and humans I had ever experienced: BTS' *Dynamite*. I played it on repeat for a month. With back rehabilitation for a suddenly slipped disc that left me barely able to walk, I savoured their smiles and glittering eyes and every thigh swerve. I stayed alive by placing myself in the middle of them, imagining a world full of so much colour and connection, dreaming of a future where I could rock those hip moves myself.

After a technicolour month of *Dynamite* on repeat, I rewatched Carpool Karaoke and became full of new questions.

Who *are* these people? That bouncy sunshine smile in the centre? The low-key jokesters in the back? The charisma oozing from Mr. Front Seat and "Mochi"? And for the love of everything right in the world, *what* is this song making my heart race? An internet search said *Black Swan*. With that, November became an endless loop of *Black Swan*, *ON*, and *Fake Love*.

When BTS released *BE*, I downloaded my first BTS songs. *Life Goes On* and *Telepathy* became daily anthems. My heart fluttered hearing them sing and seeing their faces. I created a Spotify playlist and added every song of theirs I could find. Their discography seemed bottomless and confusing, so the overwhelming playlist sat untouched over the next days. I had no idea my survival would soon depend on it.

201129

Despite 11 months of cognitive behaviour therapy and two months into mood-stabilising medication ('a wonder-drug', my psychiatrist explained), I finally lost hope on a sunny, cold November morning. I was weeping uncontrollably while recording my children riding their bicycles for the first time. My existence felt unbearably misaligned. This should be the happiest moment I had ever experienced, yet I only felt excruciating isolation while standing near my husband and watching this perfect moment unfold. My sadness was a normal part of our family, as was my husband's silence about it. It was crushing me, though. I began hyperventilating, and I left my family in the yard and disappeared into our basement.

I couldn't think clearly, only, 'I can't make my husband find me, not in his home.' The world was spinning, I was spinning. I knew I had to slow my mind. I grabbed my earbuds and thought how hearing BTS songs might literally be now or never again. I cranked the volume as high as possible to drown out the anxiety raging around me. Immediately, their voices pulled me down onto the couch, grounding me.

I don't remember what song played first. But I remember *Jamais Vu*. And *Magic Shop*. And *Begin*. *Save Me*. *Mikrokosmos*. *Stigma*. *Autumn Leaves*. And *Butterfly*. *Zero O'Clock*. *Run*. *uhgood*. And *Euphoria*. *Make It Right*. And *Interlude: Set Me Free*. A blur of variety that didn't seem like it all could possibly be from the same band. I pulled over my journal and started jotting song names as the men sang.

As they sang, I entered some sort of fairytale. Their voices somehow radiated from *inside* of me. Sparkles began floating around me. These men seemed to be singing *to me*. I could *see* them, and feel them holding me in their arms, like I was a small child. As each song changed into another, I felt seen. I felt loved.

I scolded myself. What a fool! These men didn't know me! I didn't even know *their* names or who was singing. I didn't even know what they were saying! *I really am crazy!* I berated myself.

Yet I kept being pulled back into waves of wonder by their voices. These men became my only will to live as seconds turned into hours, and morning turned into night. I just wanted to hear them sing. Another wave would gently rise, and my entire body felt weightless. Free. The next wave would crash, in bewilderment that sound could do *this*. I never before had *felt* music *in* my body, at the cellular and soul level.

We did this for eight hours. Unable to move for food, water, or the bathroom. Occasional guilt would set in that I needed to wife and mum (yes, like verbs of obligation). I would again burst into panicked tears that I needed to face the real world, and again, the men would pull me even closer into a magical world. I watched the grey sky fade into pinks, purples, and eventual darkness. I no longer felt alone. But now what?

Starting the next day, I streamed their music. Constantly. Including while I slept. My days were a mess of grief and strength, hopelessness and hope. BTS was the soundtrack.

Before the kids awoke, I researched tattoos. I had always wanted one, but most of my family felt tattoos were 'a waste of money', and I rarely made any decisions without family approval. In *those* eight hours, however, I wrote song names, the men's names, and doodles of forest, sea, and sky. I wasn't asking permission, or even discussing it. I would *not* finish 2020 without a permanent reminder of BTS giving me breath.

After the kids were asleep, I watched videos. I would add one or two videos and watch them on repeat for weeks, taking in every expression, sound, and storyline. To find music videos, I had to keep passing over fanmade videos adorning the men with hearts and rosy cheeks. I felt embarrassed thinking how teen girls must really like BTS also.

Near Christmas, YouTube steered me toward *Blood, Sweat, and Tears* and *Epiphany*, wildly different and wildly captivating. The storylines confused me, but my feelings confused me more. Watching BTS felt electric. How can BTS both go into and come from such a deep place within me? A place beyond words?

The more I watched, the more I found to watch. The more I felt, the more I found to feel. It was spiritual. After a couple weeks processing *Blood, Sweat, and Tears*, I watched a video claiming to explain it. Ten minutes later, I ordered Hermann Hesse's *Demian*. I knew then my life was forever different because of BTS, in ways that would take me years to fathom.

I loved every bit of it. I had yearned for this. Someone who was painfully soulful! Someone who believed in expressing the fullness of being human! Someone who believed sharing our truths together is how we *become* love! I not only had someone now, but *seven* someones!

I tried sharing my discoveries with people around me. Blank stares met my enthusiasm. Eventually, the replies came. 'The boy band?', 'It's a bummer it's in another language', 'I'm not a music person', and the particularly frustrating, 'I'm surprised Asian men want to look so much like girls.' How was *this* the response to my personal revival?! I found a galaxy of beauty and wonder. What I was discovering through BTS felt like my soul waking up, yet some of the people I built my entire life with, dismissed and mocked BTS... dismissed and mocked me. 'Chronic Depression Ashley' was dismissible, and it turns out, 'Excited Inspired Ashley' was, too. I suddenly felt severed into two parts, my soul into one and my physical life into another.

Just being ARMY meant experiencing more rejection, and it never stopped surprising me. Family waved it off, 'it's a phase you're in'. I enrolled in Bangtan Academy only to hear my family say, 'I think it's a weird reason to learn a new language.' For once in my life, as they ridiculed the men (and me by extension), I didn't apologise. I only grew more curious about the world and myself, even uncovering my own inner ridicule and judgments. I discovered that I am strong and courageous, determined to walk my own path with BTS beside me. For years I had lost my way, but BTS showed me I have gumption, strength, and passion. Life was so alive again, and I could feel purpose.

Day after day I was drawn in by an invisible force to watch more, and increasing numbers of fanmade videos with monikers I didn't understand and cutesy thumbnails appeared in my YouTube feed. They had become inescapable. Cringing, I wondered *what* about these grown men inspires hundreds if not *thousands* of fanmade videos. In the secret of yet another night, I surrendered to one: How Yoonmin care for each other. Oh, my heart. Inhale, exhale.

The following nights I spent all my time falling recklessly in love with these humans as I watched one fanvideo after another. These men… they're educated, brilliant artists, and also soulmates despite how wildly different they all are? Precious, playful men, inspired by life and art and each other—and their fans? They create art about loving themselves, and loving ourselves? They speak on world platforms about the intangible core of our existence: our souls! I was drinking in life through finding them.

BTS created clarity, and I realised my years of depression were because I had denied myself. I allowed myself to believe that what I wanted in life was too much, because what I wanted made my family uncomfortable. While there was nothing wrong with their desire to connect over football, breweries, and light-hearted banter, I suddenly understood that there was nothing wrong with me, either! My desire to connect over music and psychology and 'I love you's were who I am, and that isn't too much at all! God, I couldn't remember hearing a single random 'I love you' uttered to me in nearly 20 years, and hearing the men of BTS use those words were stronger than ever being called 'needy'. Why had I allowed myself to believe that I was asking for too much?

With BTS, I felt whole with the entirety of God's universe. 'Surviving until I die' was no longer an option. My walk around life was full of friction and indifference, though, and I only felt welcomed among family so long as I fought to stay in the lines of their interests. I wondered if they were happier if I stayed weak. Certain family members felt the need to call my enthusiasm into question, and my husband seemed happier making small talk with me before this expansion of myself. I was curious how scared he felt seeing me come alive at something so foreign to his own interests.

I couldn't make myself care for long periods. I needed to see and feel seen. My daily existence of tolerating companionship but not passion felt like a massive lie, which I was desperate but unable to shed. I pondered if blocking BTS might heal my marriage. Could I submit to numbness, if I simply removed evidence of my own soul again? I spiralled between knowing that who I am is fine, and continuing to believe I'm a problem to the people I love. God answered me one night as I stood under the cold moon. Under tears, I whispered, 'How do I heal, God?' Without a second between, He whispered, 'Love yourself'.

How do I do this?

The idea of BTS' 'Love myself' made me uncomfortable, so I avoided it. I loved BTS so much. I was afraid if I looked into them too hard, I would inevitably find that I don't love them. I had so many fears. What if they really are *just* a boy band? What if some members are jerks? Consequently, every step of my journey had been slowly, deliberately chosen. But I had an order from God now, right? I nervously researched the *Love Yourself* era.

Thank you, God! I could almost physically feel the synapses firing as I drank in the depth of these songs. I mapped how these songs were born from their *WINGS* era, and grew into *Map of the Soul*. Their *entire* body of work is to be human. I was overcome.

I talked with my psychiatrist, who agreed medication was not working for me because it was my life circumstances that I was unhappy with. I trashed the arsenal of sedatives and tranquillisers prescribed to me. I had my husband hide the keys to our gun safe. I fired my primary therapist, who insisted my enthusiastic but sudden changes were 'red flags' and then met with my husband to discuss what *they* thought I needed, all over again with 'go for walks' and 'wear more makeup'. I ordered *Jung's Map of the Soul*. I located a Jungian therapist in my city. I began meditating in the mornings with photos of BTS around me as support. I had decided to fight for my life, and I would not ask for anyone else's approval.

Every time I questioned if life might be easier without BTS, I remembered I had become lifeless *before* them. With BTS, I was doing the work within. It's what I wanted my entire life. It's exactly who I was meant to be, in all the right measurements. If

I were presented with an ultimatum to give up BTS, my decision was easy. BTS had walked with me, helping me define questions that had plagued my life. BTS never presented themselves as the answer. They served as lights through my own inner garden. I repeatedly learned that the answers were within me all along. BTS held my hand to remind me that I was born to discover myself, and within that journey, I would live a life worth living. They reminded me I am still worthy of love in my many facets of persona, ego, and shadow, just like I know my husband, my children, my parents, my sisters, and my brothers are. Becoming more 'me' should mean I have more to give, right?

BTS never presented an ultimatum to choose between them and anyone else. They asked me to choose myself.

By Spring 2021, I still yearned for connection with someone who understood this journey, so I poured out my struggles and appreciation for BTS online, hoping if anyone felt as lonely as I, they could find me and see they are not alone. By summer, I had met hearts from around the world, both women and men, from teens through ARMY in their 70s. I began to build actual friendships, including a special connection with a woman named Leanne. One message at a time, we discussed lyrics, loneliness, being a woman in this world, racism, dreams, and ultimately, love—all through the focal point of each of the Bangtan men and ARMY.

My walk around life might still feel desolate, but I experienced intense healing as so many of us shared our love, dreams, fears, and journeys. I believed in dreams again. I visualised travelling to South Korea with new friends. I imagined seeing Bangtan perform in 10 or 20 years, if that is how long it took to get tickets.

I ordered their entire discography to surround myself with evidence that they exist. As I first leafed through their album *BE*, a photo of Suga holding a small camera up to his eye grabbed me. I gasped as I felt him gaze at me.

As my family's unofficial photographer, I well knew the feeling of being asked to capture memories, yet rarely being in photographs myself. For years I felt useful but invisible, like no one cared to remember me, nor notice the years' worth of well-documented holidays and vacations that have little trace of me.

Yet, this. Suga wanted to photograph *me*. *I* was that important to *him*, that he desired to remember me in that very moment. I didn't care about words like 'parasocial' and 'delusional'. I burst into tears, flooded by feeling treasured. I put my fangirling shame aside and immediately placed him in a frame. I set him prominently in my living room so I could remember every day that I am loved, and that I love. My love for them and my love for myself was real, and I owed no explanation.

I suddenly saw my problem with 'boy bands' and 'fangirls' for the self-hatred it really was. My desperation to give credibility to talent, hard work, heart, perseverance, and destiny had nothing to do with validating BTS. It was a symptom of living in a societal structure built on racism, misogyny, and the internalised self-hatred of women and minorities.

The BTS self-discoveries felt eternally blooming. In spring, Jimin gave me loving eyes for my overweight, gravity-ravaged body. In summer, I experienced my first big comeback song, while we ARMY kept *Butter* at the top of industry charts for months. When BTS gifted ARMY with *Permission to Dance*, I cried in joy as I watched the men smile and bounce with abandon. I continued making ARMY friends, from the sweetest souls in Canada to Bulgaria, France to Texas, and Korea. God and YouTube introduced me to BTS, and BTS showed me the galaxy.

Healing the past

In August 2021 we arranged a family beach trip, including my older sister whom we had not seen since 2019. She moved across the world months before the pandemic, and only now was able to come back mainland. Geography had been the most recent divide between us, but circumstances were the real divide. After our Daddy's suicide, just like the case studies show, communication issues became insurmountable within our family. Our relationship faded into near non-existence. Many times over the last decade, I grieved what I felt should have been a great sister relationship. Ever since we were children, I watched how she danced through life with great heart, great curiosity, and great adventure. When I remembered our family dynamics, however, I simply wasn't willing to continue my assigned role as 'the baby', 'incapable', and 'needing protection'. I had no more patience for being the eternal damsel to anyone.

I dreaded this trip, laced with family tension, marital stress, and my inability to feel like a rightful mum (as adoption has its own set of pains to heal). I packed my earbuds and a BTS photo book, preparing to get through yet another occasion with as much numbness as I could muster. A surprise awaited me: My sister Bonnie told me she found me online. With a sparkle in her own eyes, she said I looked alive again, that I had happiness in my eyes, and she was happy that this band somehow played a role in bringing that back.

Her words were a healing balm. For months I had wondered how I could *feel* so alive and so ecstatic, yet no one except for my eldest sister Deborah had seemed to notice the change as positive. I had grown confused how becoming more alive had made me more invisible and less lovable... until now. Yes, I was alive again! And my sisters didn't shame the source. Instead, they asked me to teach them a little about these men. And Bonnie, whom I had grown so distant from, looked so full of curiosity and openness here in front of me.

I shared a few music videos. The more Bonnie watched, she asked for more. From time to time, I asked what was most fascinating to her: their artistry, their performances, or their personalities. I would ask her to point out which members held her focus in each video. Her every answer carved a path to what we would watch together next.

ARMY might be crafty, but more so, we remember that our own journey was just that — a journey. I remember seeing a reactor who tried to introduce a friend to BTS, and force the friend through what had been his own journey, as if Bangtan has only one way into our hearts, reducing ARMY and BTS to a maths equation or riddle. I felt frustrated seeing his friend look rightfully lost, as the reactor tried to explain that 'I'm Fine' spelled 'Save Me' upside down and that his friend should find that fascinating. So for Bonnie, I tried instead to be a gentle guide, letting her soul choose each direction while I helped her find footing.

In less than two days, Bonnie knew each of them by name. Initially two members stood out to her, but as she began watching personality-based content, her focus shifted. She steered her ship into choreography, cinematography, and personalities. In the spaces between, Bonnie and I related BTS into discussions of our own lives. We shared big talks about our souls, our needs, our dreams. We shared what we tolerated too long, and how we demanded more of ourselves and others now. BTS had lifted another burden from my soul. When she flew home, I accepted she may lose interest in Bangtan. But for at least those few days, we grew together in this healing energy, and I knew that would remain.

Waiting for permission

September felt like a flurry of urgency. My sister actually pursued her ARMY journey, texting me gems she found along her path, like the Bangtan Bomb of Jung Kook recording *Euphoria*, dance practices of the men dressed as Snow White and the seven dwarves, and a robed performance of *HOME*. My heart felt so full, connecting with both Bonnie and Leanne daily, and with so many new friends online. Now, my sister's journey was taking me into falling in love with the men of BTS in new ways all over again, as well as falling in love with her again, too.

Meanwhile Hybe had officially cancelled the *Map of The Soul* tour, but the good news was, the men were finally flying again! As diplomatic ambassadors of South Korea, the men were in New York, my time zone, to address the UNGA for their third time. That same day, my family suffered an unthinkable tragic death... all while BTS spoke at the MET and met with other respected artists.

Flurry. Life and emotions were flying at me from every angle and into every direction. I was the happiest I had felt in years, or maybe ever. The world was coming alive, I was coming alive, and hope was in full bloom. Yet my marriage felt more heartbreakingly alone for both of us than ever, and someone I love deeply was in the deepest grief of her life. I felt guilty for being so damn happy and full of hope. BTS felt like an affair I was having with myself, betraying other parts of my life. It was amidst this emotional chaos that Hybe announced a four-day residency in LA after Thanksgiving, a mini-tour named *Permission to Dance*. Instead of being excited, I felt deflated. The weight of knowing a concert was happening, and I wouldn't be there. The weight of fear, that I would never see them in person. That I could never thank them.

I waited a couple hours after Hybe's announcement to text my ARMY friend Leanne. I hoped she would say we should do it, and travel the entire country to see BTS together. Instead, Leanne was sad, too. We encouraged each other that the real joy is BTS finally seeing ARMY again. I insisted a world tour was surely coming, and our time would come, too. I mentioned one day travelling to South Korea to experience the home of our hearts' home.

I couldn't sleep that night. I was so terrified that we blindly consented to 'no' before even asking ourselves if going was possible. At 1:30 am, I pulled my phone under the blanket and booked a room in LA for the week of the concert. I thought my heart would beat out of my chest and wake up my whole family.

I could feel the scarlet 'A' burning across my chest, like I had just cheated on the man laying in bed next to me. I had never done anything like this before, not even close. I had to, though.

Thoughts swirled like a hurricane. 'What am I doing? Who did we need to ask, and why were or weren't we asking?' I decided I'd keep the room a secret until I also got concert tickets. If I could manage to get tickets also, then I'd tell Leanne, and figure out what to say to my husband from there.

The next morning Leanne messaged me from work, asking me to remind her all the reasons we couldn't go, and to tell her that it was absurd to imagine we could. I reluctantly confessed to booking a room and setting into motion something that might cause more stress in our lives and marriages. I could feel that I added weight onto her soul. We each had a long list of reasons not to go. I had never travelled off the East Coast, and barely left North Carolina at all. I lived in a way that if I were to experience travel, it should have been with my husband. He and I had never managed to make travel happen. Now I was going, without him, and it could cost incredible amounts of money that he had worked hard for. Besides that, Leanne and I both had realities. Health issues. Toddlers. Reasons to say no.

I just couldn't let yet another door close in my life without even trying to open it. I spent all these years looking back at closed doors with pain and regret, wishing someone had said I was allowed to open them. Fighting for my life meant breaking that pattern.

I realised the question overwhelming me was not *'How do I do this?'*, but 'what does it mean that I am doing this, that I choose this?'

We got three tickets to December 1. My sister, Leanne, and I would fly from our own corners of the globe to meet in Los Angeles. Leanne and I would meet face to face for the first time so the three of us could love on each other and these incredible souls from South Korea... and little did we know, we would also love on and be loved on by so many strangers that felt like family while we were there.

I didn't ask permission. I was terrified to ask, but I *was* going regardless of anyone else's answer. Even if I had asked as a courtesy, I would have been angry that I allowed any other person to feel that my soul was ever their decision at all. I hated that life with the man I love had become like this, but I was the one who was fighting for my life and had to do it alone.

My soul. My decision.

My yes.

211129

On November 29, 2021, I boarded my plane despite my fear of flying, heading from the East Coast to West Coast. I felt alone in my window seat, watching the runway blur as the plane lifted into the air. I hadn't put my earbuds in, but I suddenly heard Jung Kook and the first words of *Euphoria*, like he was singing beside me.

I wondered if maybe he too felt butterflies as he rose above ARMY in his Wembley performance. I quietly sobbed, thinking of Jung Kook, then Jimin. Then RM, and Jin. Suga, and j-hope, and V. I thanked God for them each. In my mind, I suddenly saw my husband's glowing smile and thanked God for the love we have shared and the playfulness we once had together, because it had been real. I saw my babies' twinkling eyes and heard their laughter. I thought about how Bangtan brought my sister Bonnie back into my inner garden, and I into hers. I wept for Leanne and myself, giving ourselves what we thought was impossible.

I cried thinking of those I come from, those I found, and those I am heading to. Bangtan was the ocean God gave me to experience life and love. I realised I didn't want to die at all but if I died on this plane before I even got there, I would die happy because I knew joy again. Bangtan had given me so much love. Bangtan gave me my heart again. As *Euphoria* continued playing through my falling tears, I thanked God for all of this, for BTS.

One year to the day after nearly ending my life, I flew to my soulmates, and to my soul. BTS invited me into the Magic Shop where I could learn how to love myself. They reminded me again and again that I never walk alone. I spent a full year studying the stars, studying the ocean, and studying the soul. I found Bangtan in all of it. Now I knew *I* was finally beginning, and I gave myself the 'yes' I spent my life waiting for. It's time to be brave. I believe in myself now. I'm different than before. And it started with a 'yes' only I could hear, only I could say, and the wings meant for me to fly.

On being found

Paola C. Rivera Santos

IT IS NO secret that life is filled with altering moments. Some go unnoticed if we're not paying attention, while others feel like a punch to the gut. Change is inevitable, it can feel involuntary, and by force at times. Life is cruel that way, it never asks you if you're okay with what is to come, you're just sort of expected to deal with the changes as they crash over you.

As a young, impressionable child, I always envisioned myself independent, self-made, self-assured, and with my shit together by the age of 27. But fantasy does not always transfer itself to reality. At 24 I was working, finishing my master's degree, and looking for a flat to rent out of my parents' home, so I could live alone. Overall, I was pretty successful, but I felt miserable. I fell into the routine of everyday life. My feelings were paralysed but life kept moving forward, and if I stopped moving I was afraid I'd drown. That's when it happened, the change, or more like a plane falling down from the sky, when your entire body tenses up as you feel the ground under you give way and gravity is pulling you down. You're defenseless, you can't do anything except wait for it all to crash. Life really can be cruel sometimes, but in this concoction of serendipity I have found myself landing in the moments where without those experiences I would have never arrived to where I am today. Despite how soul crushing the experiences have been sometimes, this version of myself would have never existed. All the beautiful moments that came with living this version of my life would have never happened. I know I am not exactly where I want to be, and I do not know where I will be in the future, but everything I do will be to honour this version of myself.

Starting high school was a particularly overwhelming time. It was a frightening transition because I was at a new school and I only knew two people, and being an introvert, adapting was not easy. I was alone, and add to that teenage angst and you've got an anxious, insecure teenager in need of an outlet. I was becoming aware of all my insecurities and how I felt so different from everyone else. I didn't listen to the same type of music as my peers. I listened to rock and pop rock. I watched too many fictional movies or shows and read fanfiction. I dressed less feminine and did not keep up with trends, so I always stood out, in a negative way. It didn't help that my girlfriends seemed to adapt easily to the new school and socialised well with our new classmates. The girls I knew exceeded academically–which I was reminded of quite frequently–and they received positive attention. I slowly started to feel like I was falling behind and did not fit in with them, or anyone. I had a hard time talking to new people; I made odd comments thinking they were funny, and felt like there was no common ground to bond with anyone there. I spent my nights playing games on my computer, reading Narnia fanfiction, watching anime, reading manga, and listening to rock music.

Looking back, none of those interests were negative, but not knowing anyone else that shared them with me, being in a new place, while also going through so many changes at times, it became overwhelming. It finally crashed down on me when we were invited to a Halloween party being hosted by one of our classmates. I remember only agreeing to go because my two friends were going. I bought a costume (I went as a Greek goddess) and my mum dropped me and one of my friends off. It gave me some peace that I was not going to arrive alone. The backyard of the house was covered with Halloween decorations and music was playing insanely loud. Some people were dancing, others were just hanging around the dance floor while talking to their friends. My friends were quickly greeted and asked to dance, while I stayed on the sidelines watching. Everywhere I looked everyone seemed to be enjoying themselves, and more importantly, like they belonged there, and I didn't. I had this invasive voice in my head that convinced me that no one wanted me around. They had no interest in getting to know me because of my different interests and lack of social skills. No one ever voiced their distaste towards me, but I was convinced they thought poorly of me.

I walked away and locked myself in the bathroom while I started to cry. I phoned and asked my mum to pick me up, but she had just dropped me off, she said it was too soon to leave. I felt like a failure, but what did I fail? Was it so wrong being who I was? At the time, I would have answered that it was.

This is where writing started to become that outlet I so desperately needed. I wrote about feeling alone, misunderstood, while also navigating my new-found physical insecurities. The pages of my journals listened to me when I could not find the words to speak to anyone about how I was feeling. Writing became the part of me I was the most sure of. In the midst of all my insecurities and internal conflicts with feeling like there was no place I could fit in, I wholeheartedly felt like writing poetry was mine and I was theirs. I felt it in my bones. It was the part of me I fell in love with, my first love.

Fast-forward several years, I finished high school but I was unsure what to do. I wanted to work while I looked at my options and thought about what I wanted to do. However, the everlasting fear of disappointing my parents pushed me into going into graduate school right after graduating from my undergraduate studies. I completed my English master's when I was 24 years old, and I still knew I wanted to be a writer. It had been the one thing I knew for certain and yet I looked at the path ahead of me and I did not recognise it. With my new master's degree I was prepared to be an educator, an English as a second language teacher. Although I did not hate it, I did not feel like it was what I was meant to be doing. I knew where I wanted to go, but my path was heading towards another direction, downhill, and I had no control. And yet, I kept walking forward. Towards the end of my master's degree I found a simple office job, which made me think to myself, 'the obvious next step is to find a small place I could call my own', thinking that maybe if I asserted this small ounce of independence from my parents, some level of control over my life would return.

On September 14, 2020, I had an unexpected feeling of being connected with my friends and hopeful for the future. I was standing on the rooftop of a nineteenth floor story building with two of my closest friends, one of them was staying with their parents who lived in that building while she visited Puerto Rico from New York. We watched the sunset, spoke about how the pandemic had affected everything, including our outlook in life and our future. Seeing the number of fatalities rise exponentially in such a short period of time, made me realise how fragile we are. No matter how much I plan for the future, nothing is certain, it was daunting. For a while the world seemed to pause, and all that followed was tragedy. How were we supposed to come back from this? I believed we wouldn't.

We stood on the edge, leaning against the short wall of cement while overlooking the smaller buildings around the one we were at. It was already nighttime, so we mostly saw the window lights and car lights in a sea of darkness. It was breezy, cool, and for a while it felt peaceful being so far away from everything. Standing so far from the ground, it made everything feel so small and meaningless. There is so much happening at the same time and yet we get caught up over the smallest issue or inconvenience, meanwhile there is a much bigger world around us. The topic of leaving Puerto Rico and living somewhere else was brought up. All three of us craved adventure and desire to explore the possibility of living somewhere else, follow our passions, see where they take us. We talked about how we knew this same desire would eventually take us away from Puerto Rico and from each other.

"Would you guys visit?" I remember asking.

"Of course," one of them said.

"This will always be home," the other one said.

It gave me a sense of peace knowing that despite how far away life would take us from one another, we always shared this place, this view, this home.

Looking back on that night, I remember wanting to imprint that moment in my brain. Who knew how long we had together. If the pandemic had taught us anything, it was that the life we knew could change as easily as flipping a switch. I wanted to remember us young and hopeful of the future before it came crashing in on us. I wanted to remember us together, high from the ground, where reality couldn't seem to touch us. I went back that night to my new apartment and wrote this poem about how I felt, wanting to solidify the memory even more:

Today I went up to a
Rooftop of a 19-
Story building in
The middle of the city with two
Friends.
I looked out into
The city lights,
Beacons calling out
To the sky
Calling out to me-

You see-

You don't always get
To choose what you
Get to remember.
Memories can be
Haunting- but when
You're given moments
Like these

Filled with freedom,
Remember them-
They'll hold you
Tight and keep you
Warm as you descend
To the ground

In the midst of my disappointment over having stopped writing to focus on a master's degree I was not passionate about, I had found a glimmer of hope that night. Looking back, even if it was just for a moment, I was content.

The next day, on September 15, 2020, midnight, I went to sleep early because of work. I was living in a small, first floor studio apartment. It had a small kitchen, a bedroom, and a bathroom. Despite having a door that separated my room from the kitchen, the space was tight and everything was close together. Still, it was my own space and I spent a few months making it feel like home. To this day I am not sure why I woke up that night, I just did. Maybe it would have been better if I had just pretended like I was asleep. Nevertheless, I woke up and the first thing I saw was the door to my room open, but that wasn't the most alarming part, on the other side the door of my apartment was also open. For a moment my entire body froze, then I felt my entire body warm up quickly. I cautiously moved towards the front door and closed it. Something was wrong and for a moment I tried to brush it off. Maybe I had not closed the doors properly and my cats pushed it open. Right beside my door I had my cat tower, where they often took naps, only this time, they were all looking towards the door of my room, intensely, defensively. I wonder if they were just as terrified as I was. I knew it then. Someone was in my room.

People often ask me why I didn't scream or run away. Well, how would you react if you woke up in the middle of the night and there was a stranger in your room? It's impossible to predict one's reaction, and I always found those questions cruel. As if I had not reacted appropriately to a man invading my apartment while not knowing his intentions. For the next hour or so, he kept me locked up in my room while he threatened to hurt me if I tried anything. He robbed me of all my personal belongings. Many praised me, called me brave over how I was able to live through that. I have always found those comments insensitive and frankly, unnecessary. It is not brave to go through a situation like this. It is not something deserving of praise and compliments. I thought I was going to die. I did not feel brave, I felt defenseless, fickle, vulnerable, and helpless. At any moment he could have become aggressive, decided to kill or sexually assault me. My fate was in someone else's hands, and I felt like it was all my fault for not being careful enough. I thought I had been ready to live alone, but I was clearly not. It is not brave to be stripped away from any sense of security, it is cruel and unfair. That night a stranger took my laptop, television, jewellery, car and above else, my ability to ever feel safe again.

After the man left in my car, I banged on the neighbour's door. I had never cried in front of strangers, but I broke down as soon as they opened the door. They had to call the police for me because I could not speak. The next few days were a blur. I mostly spent it doing police reports, retelling my incident to various police officers and investigators. It took them a few hours to find my car, it had been crashed by someone high on drugs. It was a miracle he didn't die in the crash, the car had been completely destroyed. I had to identify the man who invaded my home. Due to COVID restrictions, it had to be done through pictures, which I was grateful for. I didn't want to see him and relive that night.

I quickly moved out of the apartment and moved in with my dad and his girlfriend's family. Lucky for me, they had a spare room. It was small, cluttered, but at least I was not alone. My father got me a notebook and I painted using watercolours, it was my main source of distraction and comfort since I had no phone or computer. I barely slept. I couldn't. The slightest noise would wake me up. To this day, I still struggle to sleep some nights. The house alarm is my main source of comfort.

A few days later, I was sitting in the living room watching television. I had gotten tired of painting that day. My youngest step sister came rushing down the stairs screaming, "it's almost time!" she said as she took the television control to change the channel. I was confused, almost time for what? She confiscated the television and changed it to iHeartRadio streaming.

"BTS is performing tonight," she explained.

At that time, the only thing I knew about them was that they were a Korean band and that she and a close friend of mine adored them. I knew nothing else, not because I hated their music, I just had never gathered enough interest in listening to it. I had no energy or motivation to do anything else, so I stayed with her and watched the various performances being showcased that night. No artist stood out to me so I was having a dreadful time, hoping it would all end soon and I could go back to watching television. That all changed when BTS' turn came up. My stepsister stood up excitedly. Her excitement sparked my curiosity, I wanted to see what this group was all about since I knew she liked them so much.

The stage was decorated with bright colours, simulating a city. The camera moved slowly to the centre, focusing on the gates of an old-fashioned elevator, the ones you had to manually open. I could see my first glimpse of them through the hole of the elevator gate before they slid it open and walked out one by one. They wore vibrant colours, matching the stage. If I had to describe the look they were going for, I would have to say a modern take on the '70s. I wasn't sure what I was expecting, but it wasn't this. Maybe it was because compared to all the artists who had performed prior to them, who had generic stages and outfits, this seemed different, refreshing. Despite having to perform in front of cameras instead of a crowd of people, they put thought and effort into their stage design. My eyes moved with the camera, focusing on each one for less than a second, there was too much going on. I could feel the anticipation in me growing, heightened by my stepsister's cheers of excitement.

A high-pitched pop voice started to sing, "'Cause I, I, I'm in the stars tonight,"[1] the first verse of the song. The camera honed in on one of the band members, he was at the centre, he had ruffled black hair with a suit of the same colour with white, vertical lines. He opened the song with a huge smile on his face, it radiated confidence, like he knew what was coming was a top-tier performance. It was contagious. I felt enjoyment for the first time in days. To my surprise, my stepsister followed their choreography naturally. I later learned that this is something ARMY does for fun. I am not sure if it was their upbeat music, charisma, choreography, or overall stage presence that left me in awe, but I could not take my eyes off the screen. For the entirety of the four songs they performed, I was completely enthralled by them. Never had I heard a single song by them, and yet, there I was completely mesmerised by their music. Something had clicked inside my brain. For the first time in days, I had felt something that was not rooted in fear or helplessness. I felt hope.

I was fortunate enough to have a close friend who liked them, so for the next few days I mostly asked her questions and she tried to update me on seven years' worth of memories, information, and music. I wanted to know about their beginnings, how they created the group, what were the best songs or the first ones I should listen to. I wanted to know about who they were as individuals. She shared with me important interviews, achievements, and music videos all in the span of a few days. It was a rollercoaster. There seemed to not be enough hours in the day to properly catch up with their journey while simultaneously starting my own with them. They had debuted over seven years prior, and I had just started to get familiar with them. How could I possibly catch up while also getting to know them in my own way? My journey had started late, but it felt destined, and perfect. It was thrilling, and it helped take my mind away from what had happened. It was escapism at its best. Arguably, escapism is not always the best remedy, but they filled my dreadful days with joy, and gave me tranquillity when it was time to go to sleep.

They shortly announced an online concert (*ON:E*) for October 10 and 11, 2020. I convinced two friends to watch it with me. I stayed over at my ARMY friend's house. I felt like a child, unable to sleep, giddy over the excitement to watch them perform. We bought takeout, and she spent a few hours showing me more videos and talking about them with me. She even took out her album collection and let me flip through them and explained what photocards were. My bias was (and still is) Jimin. She had a photocard of him and decided to gift it to me, it was from their *Love Yourself: Answer* album. I kept it in my wallet for months before I found out how to properly take care of photocards. It is now inside a frame displayed in my drawer and travels with me. By this time I was only familiar with less than five songs by them, so I was unsure of what to expect. Despite consuming as much content in the weeks leading up to the concert, I had only listened to a handful of songs on repeat. Looking back, I am glad I got to experience so many songs for the first time through that concert instead of listening to their music through their albums. Watching them perform live, even through a screen, it felt like a more pure experience than the albums would have ever given me. Beyond their professionalism and overall stage presence, I was able to experience the energy of each song through their performances. My favourite part was seeing them enjoying themselves while performing together. It reminded me of the same energy I felt when Jung Kook smiled the first time I saw them performing. In fact, I did not even know they had solo and unit songs so imagine my surprise when RM came on stage and sang *Intro: Persona* or when RM, j-hope, and Suga started to perform *UGH!*, which was such a hype song, it made me want to stand up and dance (it was 6:00 a.m. and we had to be quiet because of my friend's sleeping boyfriend). When Jimin's *Filter* performance came out I had to stand up, I could not remain seated. I am pretty sure I watched the entire performance with my mouth open. I am not exaggerating when I say I fell to my knees when he sang the bridge of the song. From day one, he had been the member that had consistently caught my attention. His sultry voice had something haunting but soothing about it, his dance, the way he moved entrapped me and wouldn't allow me to look away. I believed that whatever he was feeling while performing, I could feel it too. The way he poured himself into his art resonated with how much I would also pour myself into mine.

Each solo and unit performance was unique and different from the next, it felt like smaller concerts. Each one of them had unique styles and they highlighted it with their performances, making it their own. They somehow were able to perform together and at the same time as individuals while simultaneously still being part of BTS. Their range in talent was enough to leave anyone impressed, but I felt mostly inspired. They projected so much creativity, it made me want to start creating as well and I think that is what made me get attached to them so quickly. By the end of the first concert, I knew with certainty I was in this for the long haul. I bought a ticket for the second day on the spot. I needed more, despite having to wake up at 4:30 a.m. to watch it.

The concerts ended, and I was left on a high. What I had witnessed had not only been an exemplary showcase of high quality artistry, but an explosion of emotions. I laughed, I danced, I felt amazed, stunned, heartbroken, and hopeful. It almost felt like a release from everything I had been feeling for the last few weeks. For the first time in a while, I was once again reconnecting with feeling excitement while still trying to heal. I was not only revitalised by their music, but by their words of encouragement and vulnerability.

For the next few weeks I had to talk to a public defender and give out my statement of the assault. They asked me to be as detailed as I could be. I helped with the written statement. Every time I was forced to relive that night I would go back to listening to BTS' music, I would replay the concert in my head and how happy I felt while watching it and tried to hold on to that feeling. A song I listened to quite often was *Spring Day*. Aside from the beautiful musical composition, I held on to the promise it gave that winter didn't last forever, and that I would also see spring again. It was the feeling of hope they had given, compressed into one song. A hope that if I had not found, I do not know how I would have navigated the recent events of my life. On October 26, 2020, I had to go to court and be witness to the sentencing of my attacker. I remember sitting in court, humming BTS lyrics to myself while fidgeting with my fingers as I tried to calm down the nerves.

It was over.

For the months to come, I grew closer to BTS' music as I learned more about their song lyrics and messages. I found a surge of inspiration. I had an old love I had neglected for too long, and it needed mending. They started me on a path of trying to forgive myself for abandoning that side of me and towards healing and reconciling that relationship with myself. Seeing BTS' commitment to their music made me want to share my voice again. The lyrics "You found me, you knew me, you gave me the best of me so you'll give you the best of you"[2] often remind me of what BTS means to me. It never felt like I found them, instead, they found me when I needed them the most, they opened up the doors to the magic shop and let me in so I could be safe. Now I want to show them the best of me, I want to find peace again, and I want to love myself as much as I love them.

I started to write again, by re-learning and familiarising myself with that side of me I had let go of for a long time. Although I am still not exactly where I feel like I am meant to be, I know that being found by BTS felt right, predestined. It was like new air was pushed into my lungs, and I was able to breathe freely for the first time in years. Shortly after finding them I wrote 300 pages in less than two months, my first draft of a novel and I started drafting a poetry book. I revisited some old journals and worked on editing old poems. I quit my toxic job and also worked on finishing my master's thesis. I cried so much the night I did, out of relief mostly. Still, a part of me was sad I could not let BTS know that I did it, I finally did it, and it was in part thanks to them.

I can say that if it hadn't been for my stepsister hijacking the television that night, I would have not found the smallest ember of hope I now carry with me everywhere. I am still not sure what it was that made me stay that night to watch them perform. Maybe it was the fact that I had nothing else to do, or maybe it was just meant to happen this way. Life worked its magic and brought them to me when I needed them the most, destiny can be interesting like that. Looking back, there were many opportunities where I could have learned who they were before I did, and yet, it had to be then. I am glad life had the perfect moment saved up for our paths to cross. Who knew that such a small, mindless decision to wait for their performance would lead to one of the best decisions I have ever made. Sometimes life changes in the most predestined way, sometimes it's a huge impactful moment, and other times it's small, like buying a journal on a whim or deciding to stay with your stepsister while she watches a music show. For whatever reason these changes happen, they are irreversible and permanent. Despite the pain, I am who I am because of all that I have been through, and I am thankful BTS found me, in spite of the circumstances, and brought me home to the magic shop.

It is hard to explain how BTS reshaped my life. It almost sounds absurd that a band composed of seven men I have never met could improve anyone's life. At the end of the first day for the *ON:E* concert I watched, RM said, "We are literally strong. The ARMY that I know and the BTS that everyone knows, we are all strong. We will find a way, we always have. If there is no way, let's draw the map, the whole map again"[3] I couldn't stop crying over how overwhelmed I felt at that moment. I knew he was talking about COVID, and yet the words meant something else for me. Here I was, being told by a stranger, that everything was going to be okay. I believed him, I felt like it was true. It was the sincerity in his voice and the pain in his eyes that just like me, he was suffering as well. In that struggle and suffering, I felt connected to him, even if through a screen and music. As a writer, I know the weight of words, and the power they hold. As a writer, BTS were the muse I had been waiting for, the motivation to reunite with the love I had put away because I had believed it wasn't enough for the world. But they showed me that it was enough—I was enough. My voice, my words, my imperfect beautiful being had always existed, I just had to embrace her. I knew the only way I could was through my writing, the truest of loves I had ever felt. And so, I now walk through life, learning who I am and who I am to become with BTS cheering me on, just as I cheer for them.

References

[1] BTS. (2020). Dynamite [Song]. On *BE* [Album]. Big Hit Entertainment.

[2] BTS. (2018). Magic Shop [Song]. On *Love yourself: Tear* [Album]. Big Hit Entertainment.

[3] Zhenrickavl. (2020, December 14). *Namjoon's message during Map of the Soul :One online concert |RM|* [Video]. YouTube. https://youtu.be/i3ehyFudg-k

Seven points in my narrative's universe

M. Anastasia Kinderman

WHEN WALLEA ASKED me if I'd like to include a chapter in this book I was initially hesitant, but not necessarily for the reasons one might think. It's difficult for me to express in words the impact BTS has had on my life. When I try, the words come out empty, and fall short of expressing what I want to.

There's also the fact that expressing the impact sometimes requires giving voice to pain I don't usually talk about, or that I brush off to make it seem less serious. Talking about healing requires an explanation of what I'm healing *from*, and sometimes I'm not even sure how to properly put some of my experiences into words.

It's not that I'm ashamed of what I've been put through, it's that sometimes I doubt people's ability to fully understand (through no fault of their own). I feel like some of it is, at times, almost unbelievable.

But I have many friends that are ARMY, and many of them have told me their stories and struggles. They are not outliers. Throughout these pages, almost every author has mentioned the oft quoted saying we have in our fandom: You find them when you need them the most. We say it so much because it's true. As it is for me, so it is for others.

I'm tired of not having the depth of meaning I intend behind the words "I am ARMY" properly communicated. And I rejoice when people connect with the fandom and realise that they are not alone, that others share their pain, that this is a safe place to heal.

In that vein, this is my attempt to add yet one more story to the living proof of the revolution we are in.

Permission to live

When a person comes from a background where they're expected to box themselves up and fit into one mold, it's easy for them to believe there are things they don't deserve. When a person has lived their whole life in survival mode, it can be hard to see when it's no longer necessary. It's easy to dream and wish, but be too afraid to actually make things happen.

Once upon a time, this was my life. My doubts and fears were brushed away as quickly as they came. I was afraid that the people around me would be able to somehow discern my thoughts and see my disbelief, my rebellion, and that I would suffer the consequences.

Yet here I sit today, a completely different person than the one who existed several years ago. There is a drastic, discernible difference.

What happened to split my life into these two parts, what finally got me to live? The short answer is BTS.

The longer answer is that I reached a point in my life, despite my fears and the restrictions placed on me, where I could not remain in my box any more. I would say I was primed and ready, but it was more like I'd been betrayed and broken down to the tiniest pieces of myself. Everything I thought was certain was gone, and I was left with a smarting heart that constantly reminded me of what had been taken. Now I was lost and trying to figure out how to rebuild.

It was not an overnight thing. This kind of stress can drive a person back into the simple expressions of comfort, and for me that was the hard beats and amazing dance performances that K-pop offers.[1] It felt like a momentary relief from all the topsy-turviness, and I wanted more of this temporary balm. In my search for new bands to listen to, it did not take long for YouTube to recommend BTS to me. While I didn't know much about them (or any of the other artists I encountered), they stuck with me. They stayed on repeat. They immediately became one of the first bands I listed when people asked me who my favorite Korean idols were. There was just something about their story lines, their lyrics, and even their beats that entertained, yes, but also comforted. It was the perfect soundtrack to play while recreating my life.

It could be said it was a coincidence that I came across them, it could also be said it was a divine meeting orchestrated by the universe.[2] Whatever viewpoint you come from, the beginning of me today was at that moment in time. I could say I built her myself, but that would be a lie. While, in the end, it was my drive that propelled me on this new path, I could not have sustained it without the support of my family, friends, and BTS and their music. The current existence of my identity is intertwined with the things I have learned and the comfort I have gained from all of them.

For every hard decision I have made, there is a memory of playing a BTS song on repeat as I struggled with what to choose. For every depressive episode, there are songs I have played over and over while I waited for the chemicals in my brain to realign. For every doubt and struggle, there are the members' voices expressing the same doubts and struggles, leaving me feeling less alone.

Their songs, their example, themselves, all worked together to give me the permission I felt I needed to get out and live.

After all, if you're not alive, you can't dance.

More specifically, I think my story can be divided into seven (ha!) points in time that I believe might have a chance of properly communicating what I really mean when I say "I am ARMY". When you hear me identify myself, I mean more than just "I am a fan". I mean that my current existence would be impossible if they also did not exist.

#1 Pursue my dreams

Earlier, I mentioned how I feel like BTS gave me permission to live. By this, I mean that choosing to and actually living my life did not seem possible for someone like me, at one point. I was raised in a pessimistic environment. The example set for me was to dream and then sabotage, ultimately proving my unworthiness to both myself and the people surrounding me. If I did dare to defy this and dream, giving voice to those dreams ultimately resulted in them being shot down or me being traumatised in their pursuit. A constant companion of mine was hopelessness.

In my late teens, one of my most precious dreams was that of education. Despite the propaganda I was routinely subjected to—that women existed to serve men and thus there was no need for me to be educated, that education was from the devil to lead me astray, that I didn't need a degree to birth out as many kids as possible so why bother—I envisioned myself becoming "normal" and having the quintessential American experience. Turning 18, leaving for college, four years of immersing myself in studies, graduating with a ton of debt, finding a good job somehow and paying it all off, and so on.

Perhaps because I was raised in it, the full depths of the contempt towards women that both my father and some of the people I was surrounded by did not register. And the pure hatred that they rain down on women who step out of line I also didn't fully comprehend. What began as an expressed innocent desire to attend college and, even worse, study psychology, eventually morphed into a several month campaign of terror directed at me. Not only was I fighting myself internally, the years of hopelessness and self-sabotage taking their toll, but other people were brought in to warn me of the dangers of thinking for myself and the necessity of submitting to my father's desires. I was routinely sat down in my father's office, called nasty names, and threatened with horrible things. His screaming sessions would go on for hours, and twice ended with him determinedly leaving to get his gun and 'take care of' the problem he was presented with. Me.

I remember sitting there and being petrified, unable to move, with a sinking realisation that I was trapped and had no way out. If I ran for my life, everyone we knew would be on his side and no one would help me. I would be truly alone, with no way to support myself, ostracised from everyone I knew, and I was not capable of handling those burdens. My only option was to wait for him to come back down the stairs and put a bullet in my head, because I had nowhere else to go. Each second seemed too slow but also too fast as I mentally pulled back and just... gave up.

Even when I heard his footsteps coming back down the stairs, I could barely muster the energy to care. I couldn't mentally handle that amount of terror for the amount of time he had kept me waiting, so when he came to the door and I realised he'd changed his mind, I didn't experience a flood of relief. I just thought it was nice I could go to bed and not interact with people for the rest of the night.

Because of this incident, as well as others, I think it is understandable that while I eventually did follow my dream in some capacity, there was a reluctance on my part to follow through with any others. Even though I was now an adult, the powerful reasoning of "following your dream = pain and suffering" was still substantial. This is where BTS comes in, because a year after I had first found them, they began helping me confront this reluctance.

After, finally, obtaining my degree, I had toyed with leaving my employment and wanted to travel. But I was scared to take the steps required to actually chase these dreams, and allowed them to sit in my head wistfully instead. I longed to follow those dreams, but found excuses for why I shouldn't even try. Defeating myself before others could.

When the *Burn the Stage* documentary was released, I saw it as an opportunity to learn more about the band whose music I found so comforting. What really hit home for me while watching was how dedicated they were to their dreams, how much it meant to them to succeed. They didn't coast, they actively worked and didn't stop till they got what they wanted. It was impressive. It was inspiring.

For once, I asked myself, 'Why can't I do that?' Rationally, what was preventing me from pursuing *my* dreams now? I realised I had a choice, but I did have to choose. I could face my fears and start working towards my goals, or I could give up and stay in my comfort zone. But if I gave up, I'd have to stop dreaming. I saw it as pointless to wish for change if I didn't plan to actually make it happen.

I imagined myself at the end of my life. Which option would I wish I'd chosen? Which option would leave me with the least regrets?

I chose. And I have not stopped choosing that option since.

#2 Getting off the seesaw

Because I had known nothing else, it has taken me a long time to understand how abusive the situation I was raised in was. The dynamics of trauma bonding, the fear when someone is inevitably angry and the relief felt when they eventually calm down, are as intimate to me as the air I breathe.

Because of the slow change in my social circles, I was mostly supported when I began pursuing my dream of moving abroad, which bolstered my courage in making this decision. Alone it was scary and I second-guessed myself, but with friends and family telling me I could do it? It still seemed scary, but now conquerable. Now it was a challenge, not an enemy.

But several months before I finally got on the plane, my father had a change of heart and began going out of his way to needle at and provoke me. What was supposed to be a happy time for me, excitement at the coming change as I invested time with my family and friends, morphed into dread as I would wake up and wonder what he was going to do *this time* to try and get a rise out of me.

I would get in my car after interactions with him and just cry, because I was trying so hard to have a good relationship with him, I did want that, and it felt like all he was doing was sabotaging my efforts. He would say the cruelest, most hurtful things, and then he'd ask me if I was planning on cutting all contact with him when I moved (making me promise not to), or accused me of intending to. While I hadn't initially, he began to make the option look incredibly tempting. I felt like I was trying to reach an impossible standard, and I grew more and more frustrated as all my efforts were mocked or completely disregarded. Nothing I did was good enough, and he made sure I felt that every day up until the day I left.

My drives around town were usually accompanied, at that point in time, by *FAKE LOVE* or *Seesaw* on repeat because I felt like they fully encapsulated my grief at what I was experiencing. I felt like he didn't actually love me, he loved this image that he wanted me to be, that I was incapable of being. And it felt like my excitement at achieving one of my dreams had morphed into a desire to escape, to finally get away from the arguments and the petty, cutting swipes at my character. I resented that he had turned what should've been a good experience into something that made me feel like I was running away. I had never wanted to be that kind of person. I don't run from my problems. And yet only physically removing myself, getting off the seesaw, would finally stop this back and forth.

What cemented this need to, once and for all, stop the up and down in its tracks, was me accompanying him on a six-hour drive in a blizzard to a small, rural town for a funeral. It was exhausting as I am an introvert, and he is a talkative extrovert. I foolishly still believed him when he said he wanted a good father-daughter relationship. He proceeded to take advantage of that belief, locking me in our hotel room and preventing me from leaving. Subjecting me to hurtful accusations and name-calling until I broke down crying, then blaming his behaviour on the fact that we were "too different" as if difference had ever prevented me from being able to connect with others. The problem wasn't difference, the problem was a lack of respect for me as a human with personhood. I knew now I deserved that respect, but once again I was stuck and couldn't get away. I could only take his emotions as they were thrown at me and wait for it to end.

That was the last straw. Just weeks later, when I stepped on the plane to fly to my new home, I left knowing that I had tried everything possible to salvage what I thought we had. I left with no guilt. When I got off our seesaw, when I made that hard decision, it was with the knowledge that I had done my best. I was sad, yes, but now also mature enough to know the blame rested squarely on his shoulders. As the plane lifted off, I played *Seesaw*, trying to not cry from the great loss I felt inside.

#3 Accept myself

It's probably easy to guess why I might struggle with who I am, and with being okay with that person. I have always compared myself to others, and fallen short. The lack of opportunities when I was younger made me feel restricted and behind my peers. Even today, I still find myself lacking in knowledge I feel I should possess and it makes me feel self-conscious.

My chief desire as a little girl was to fit in. I didn't want to be the dowdy girl wearing the jean skirts and tennis shoes, who doesn't know how to colour-coordinate. I wanted to read fashion magazines, talk to boys (because I was in denial about my other attraction), wear makeup, and watch the popular shows on Disney Channel. As a teenager, I both desired yet resented the (at first, few) times I was let out of the house, almost always with a chaperone, as I tended to overdress since wearing skirts outside of the home was a requirement. I shrank under the judging glances and occasional comments directed my way, which always made me feel like I was an ugly, walking disaster. I just wanted to look pretty and feel good, and those were two things apparently not in the cards for me.

If I had been older, perhaps I would have been able to see that I wasn't the problem, my environment was. I could've placed the blame where it belonged, instead of absorbing it in splotches of shame through my skin. But I was young and this was all I'd ever known, and girls who spoke up and out of turn were made into examples for the others. I blamed myself, for being ugly and supposedly always needing supervision, for having no sense of style. I internalised it, I felt shame, and I hated myself.

It makes sense then that, once I got any measure of freedom, my chief desire was to find a way to fit in. That was all I thought I wanted. But I eventually found that I had jumped from one box into another. My original box silenced me, tried to make me dependent, shamed me for having thoughts that weren't in line with the people surrounding me. My new box judged me for my lack of pop culture knowledge, my nerdy interests, work ethic, and lack of interest in partying. I got my chance to fit in and found I still didn't fit, and now I thought it was also overrated.

Hearing the members' stories as they've journeyed to accept themselves and each other, legitimised my pursuit of myself. Many ARMY will remember the infamous incident where RM and Suga were berated on a radio show by a fellow rapper, who harshly judged them for joining an idol group.[3] Perhaps because they had made different choices, this other man felt insecure and took it out on them. While I'm not happy they were put through that, it makes any words they say about acceptance of oneself and not caring what others think ring with the sound of experience. It makes it easier to hear their words, because I know they too have felt this shame I have felt.

BTS has always been different, and that's partially the reason for their success. It took me some time to realise it, but just because I am also different from other people in some things, doesn't mean I'm "bad" (or that they are, also). It's okay to be me, and I can rest in that knowledge.

#4 Better myself

For many years, I felt not good enough. I've felt like there was something horribly ugly and wrong with me, and I couldn't rest until I fixed it. I would take constructive criticism hard, so hard that it became a self-attack on me as a person. Instead of fighting back, I used those words as weapons to justify my self-hatred and self-flagellation.

In the betrayal that occurred right before I found BTS' music, many accusations were levelled against me. Some were true, some weren't. I had grown up having innocent actions twisted into accusations of horribleness. Well-meaning actions suddenly blew up in my face, and I was painted as a horrible monster with evil intentions I hadn't known motivating me. If that wasn't enough, on my own, I saw many things in myself I didn't like.

As a result, I became obsessed with character development. I felt behind, like everyone else was a good person and I wasn't, and I also had a long way to go on top of that. I had so many things to learn, so much catching up to do to become a decent person. It was exhausting and often made me feel desperate as I strived to rid myself of self-hatred in this way.

Now, I am not saying character development is bad. What I am saying is that I had the wrong mindset towards it. Character growth is a journey, not a quick hop and a skip. Ideally we will always be growing and learning, and we will never fossilise and become grumpy, old people with no imagination.

BTS' openness and attitude towards their flaws is encouraging. They don't deny they have them, but they work on them. And they don't let them impact their image of themselves. Through watching interviews and other content, I would see them list things they wanted to change, while also praising themselves when they succeeded. An example of this would be 2019's New Year Bangtan Bomb, where BTS wishes ARMY a happy new year. Jung Kook admitted he had made lots of 'promises' to himself that he didn't keep, but rather than beat himself up he decided he would try again in the new year.[4]

Sometimes the things they want to work on would be stuff that had never occurred to me. This would be like when Jin made comments about the idea of rest and what it entails. Jin considers not being productive and being "lazy" to be an important component of resting properly.[5] When reading his interview on this in *Vogue*, I realised it had never occurred to me to interrogate my own definition of the word 'rest' and how I go about it. It made me wonder if this was something I needed to explore more. But not only that, even when he discusses how he can improve, he doesn't treat himself like he's worthless until he reaches this goal.[6] He's still worthy even though he's not perfect.

BTS have a 'we will always be working on ourselves' attitude, and it's reflected in their music. A common theme in their discography is change, and how we are different people at different points in time. This is not bad, this is simply what is.

They have both encouraged me to continue developing my character, and helped me realise that it is a journey I shouldn't shame myself for.

#5 Speak myself

Of course, BTS is known for encouraging people, especially ARMY, to raise their voices and speak their truth. But I want to talk about some other nuances I have seen them display.

Upon initially getting out into the big, wide world, I was shocked that people would listen to me. I was used to having to fight to be heard, being misunderstood and having to over explain, having to make every detail of my statements 'correct' or it being brushed aside. As a woman in the misogynistic circles I was in, I had to be careful to always come off as logical and rational, even as the men I engaged with displayed extremely emotional behaviors, because if I didn't... that was it. Nothing I'd say would matter, I would be dismissed as just another woman who was emotional and this is why women should not be listened to.

When I found myself in environments where it wasn't a constant battle, I readily gave into the temptation to talk too much. If I'm not going to receive punishment and backlash for speaking, it made sense to finally get all my words out! If someone says something inaccurate, why can't I correct them?

BTS, especially initially in their career, were definitely not strangers to speaking up for themselves. They said what they thought, and there was plenty of criticism. I don't want to say that they no longer do so, but I think we can see an evolution in how they go about it. Sometimes, now, BTS... just says nothing. When unfair articles are published about them, their main account doesn't retweet it, and that's about it. The silence sends a message that BTS is too busy doing important things to bother with the jealous drama people attempt to start. RM himself has even told ARMY to ignore when haters speak about them, that they're not worth the energy.[7]

At other times, they suavely bring a conversation around to an issue and address it, but in a way designed to keep things smooth. I saw RM do this when he took a jab at news coverage of ARMY online activity, assuring the interviewer BTS had come to the U.S. to see actual people and not "robots" when they were in the U.S. for the L.A. PTD concerts.[8] I also saw it when RM, speaking for the other members as well as himself, confronted James Corden over jokes Corden made that came off as mocking the fandom. Despite BTS' smiles, they understood how hurtful the jokes had been for the fandom and spoke on our behalf to get an apology.[9]

In other cases, we see them wait and address it in their music. More recently, this has been displayed with *UGH!*, when the rap line expresses their "outrage" at "malicious anger" on the internet they feel needs "to be put down".[10] In *Run BTS* also, they take the opportunity to list their hard work and accomplishments, with RM sparing one line to say "U said u hot, oh man, u not".[11] This is, of course, not limited to only group albums, as it can be dealt with in their solo work as well. This is the case in *What Do You Think*, where Suga may not name names but he gives his opinion on the haters, calling them "delusional" and "little brats" among other choice words.[12]

Seeing this, then, my understanding of what 'speak yourself' means has changed since I first encountered the concept. I no longer see it as just being able to talk and say what I think, I also see it as *when* and *who* I talk to. Not everyone is deserving of the energy it takes me to engage with them. It's important to me that when I speak, I'm listened to and taken seriously. If I'm surrounded by people who just want to hear their own voices, it's a waste of my energy to shout into that void. I don't see it as being silenced, I see it as saving my energy for the people and situations where I know my voice will be heard.

A good example of this would be arguing with someone over whether women have human rights, a topic that would obviously come up in my background. Could I make some good arguments on this subject? Oh, yes. But if I'm faced with someone who is open to debating this, that already tells me that they're not worth my time. The fact that they consider this up for debate shows they won't be willing to listen to me. My breath will be wasted on someone who can't appreciate the time and energy I've put into creating my arguments and, honestly, who probably won't be on my intellectual level. In a case like that, am I really speaking myself? Or getting dragged into an argument that I'm being set up to fail at, having my energy drained and wasted?

Sometimes the best thing I can do is walk away, show someone that what they're saying is so ridiculous I don't even have time for it. Sometimes, silence can speak the loudest.

#6 See my worth

Accepting myself, bettering myself, and speaking myself can all be seen as aspects of realising my worth. And BTS has helped greatly with this. I can't say it's a journey that is over for me, but it is one that I have made progress on.

It can't be underestimated the damage that is done when a woman is raised in an environment that both holds her in contempt and hates her. I was seen as the ultimate root of all evil, taught that knowledge is corrupting, that original and/or angry thoughts are temptations to fight, that my body is impure and I am in constant danger from every man around me, that my main purpose is to first serve my father and then husband (preferably as early as possible), that my worth is in my womb, and that I am a lesser human who should feel shame for existing as my gender. That domestic violence, child molestation, and rape are the woman's fault, and it is on her to 'fix things', 'make it right', and repent. After all, a man would not hit a woman if she was submitting, and a woman wouldn't be touched so inappropriately if she weren't behaving in a manner designed to tempt.[13,14,15]

I hated myself for existing in a woman's body, and I cried at how unfair it was that my gender sentenced me to killing off the parts of myself that made me, me, so I could spend the rest of my life building up some pathetic man who wouldn't get anything done without my abilities.

I think it's understandable, then, how I have found both BTS' actions and their music healing in this area. When given opportunities to mock their (mostly female) fans, I saw them refuse to contribute to the "crazy" and "weird" narrative.[16] When they were criticised for perceived misogynistic lyrics in songs like *War of Hormone*, I saw them admit they were wrong and educate themselves so it wouldn't happen again.[17] The 'feminist hit list' website that was uploaded before the Korean presidential election, by the current president's young, male supporters, featured only several men, one of whom was RM.[18] I have seen them buy and wear products related to women's issues, such as their own country's comfort women, and supported women-owned businesses in South Africa and the UK.[19,20,21] I have seen them reach out to female artists in the music industry, and definitely noticed their respectful behavior towards those same women.[22,23,24]

And then there are their songs, where I've listened to them speak of their love for their fans (many women) with lyrics like "you're the best to me just the way you are",[25] how much all our support means to them as they brag that they "got ARMY right behind us when we say so",[26] how they want to walk this path with us so we "are not alone",[27] and how they will always be there for us when they say "you and I, best moment is yet to come".[28]

They have become my safe space when I still encounter vestiges of what I grew up in, they are who I reach for when the hatred for my existence becomes too much to bear. They are a comforting reminder that what I was taught is a lie and that life is so much better than what I was told.

#7 Enforce boundaries

Many BTS songs hold a special place in my heart, and I'm hard-pressed to pick a favorite (sorry, song Twitter), but *ON* and *Butter* definitely stand out in the story of my life. Six days after the release of *Butter*, I groggily woke up to frantic messages and calls from family and friends. While I had escaped my father's clutches and now had minimal contact with him, that was not the same for several other members of my family as they attempted to navigate abusive headspaces, religious doctrine, and everyday life. It was my worst fear come true, my father had attacked two of my sisters, and the fact that neither died is most likely due to the quick actions of one of them.

Anyone who has had someone they care about in an abusive situation can understand how frustrating it is when that person is still caught up in the cycle of abuse. Yes, many of us have also been there at one point, but now we see what's so obvious and wish others would spare themselves the pain and skip the mental journey we've made. I found myself overwhelmed. Not only was I attempting to process my own anger and trauma, but also helping my siblings with theirs, and advising my family on the next steps to take.

It felt like my life had ground to a halt as I processed my shock, and yet the world required me to keep going and be responsible. I moved back and forth between working on my final papers for the semester and texting my sisters, with *Butter* playing in the background as my only tie to a fragile reality. A reality where I was no longer a scared teenager but instead a frustrated woman.

Unsurprisingly, when someone has existed in patriarchal circles that teach entitlement to things simply because they're male, there is bound to be a lack of self-awareness. My father did not see these events, that to us were monumental, as being that big of a deal. In fact, we were overreacting and resisting godly submission to him, in his eyes. Since I had become so withdrawn, and had given my father some hard truths since leaving, perhaps I became something like the forbidden fruit, something he no longer possessed and wanted back. Or maybe he really is just that delusional. In any case, his actions forced a final, abrupt realisation that he would never change. All his promises were empty, there was no hope, and he had to understand that actions have consequences. I had reached the end of our journey, despite all my efforts, and there was simply no way to 'make' him love us. There was only protecting the people *I* loved from this point on.

I was sitting in a trendy cafe, overlooking some beautiful, crystal blue water, when my finger hesitated over the send button. It had taken me a month to write this email. I had read it, reread it, rewritten it, had friends give me feedback, had my family give me feedback, but at some point I needed to sit down. I needed to make this final. That morning, I had gotten the final piece of feedback I needed.

I had *ON* on repeat, to give me strength, to remind myself of all I'd been through and that, ultimately, things would eventually be okay. I read it again. And again. I had to rest one hand on my thigh to hide the fact that my whole body was trembling. A small part of me was screaming that this was it, that if I sent this there was no going back. This was the end.

Those tempting small traces of my old trauma bond tugged on my mind, arguing to put it off a little longer. Once I sent it, I couldn't go back. It would be done. I questioned if I would regret it, for the millionth time.

The other part of my mind reminded me of my desire to live without regrets. To protect and show I valued the people I said I cared about. That this may hurt my heart, but there was no progress without pain. This is what BTS has shown me over the years. That part of my mind reminded me of what I wanted, freedom. And I hit send.

I sent my father a letter cutting off contact, with an explanation for when he inevitably tries to smear my name to anyone who will listen. I doubt he understands the significance, but in one of the last lines I told him I didn't need his permission to dance.

BTS' support had shown me I only, ultimately, need my own.

"I am ARMY"

I think sometimes ARMY is seen as a puzzle, people do not understand where our passion comes from. Some respect it, some denigrate it. I believe this is partially because of assumptions made and a lack of listening. It is assumed we're bots. It is assumed we're emotional hysterics who foam at the mouth when we see BTS in tight pants. It is assumed that we're just extremely dedicated to the seven sexual objects we consume. And maybe there are some. Maybe there is an ARMY account on Twitter that is really a bot. There are definitely some people in the fandom who don't stop to fact-check before blasting away, uncaring of the collateral damage. And yes, I have seen some people who have nothing better to do but attempt to sexually harass the members on Weverse and say BTS should be happy to be objectified because they're Asian.

But they are not the majority. It is nothing more than a lazy smear campaign to paint us all like that. To understand where our passion comes from, look at our stories. As I said at the beginning, many of us have painful stories. Many of us have found healing with these seven men and within this fandom.

Like other ARMY, I have been given much and learned much from BTS. I am sure that this is still early in this together journey, and that I will learn more and heal more in the future. When I do though, I know there is one thing that will stay consistent. My ability to convey what I mean when I say "I am ARMY" will still feel inadequate, but the story will be much longer.

References

1 Ducharme, J. (2020). *Why you're regressing to your teenage self during COVID-19*. Time. https://time.com/5819224/covid-19-act-like-teeangers/

2 BTS. (2017). DNA [Song]. On *Love Yourself: Her*. Big Hit Entertainment.; Doolset. (2018, June 30). *DNA* [Translation]. https://doolsetbangtan.wordpress.com/2018/06/30/dna/

3 The Korean Times. (2019). *Rapper says sorry for slamming BTS amid fans' rage*. South China Morning Post. https://www.scmp.com/lifestyle/entertainment/article/3019143/rapper-b-free-says-sorry-bts-slamming-them-interview-six

4 Bangtan Subs. (2019, Jan 2). *[BANGTAN BOMB] Happy new year 2019!* [Video]. YouTube. https://www.youtube.com/watch?v=skLnf1Z2_dM

5 Kwon, M. (2022). *BTS's Jin on rest, the importance of uselessness and his unique philosophy of fun*. Vogue Singapore. https://vogue.sg/bts-jin-vogue-singapore-cover-interview/

6 Ho, S. (2021). *Jin: "A New Year's message of hope for all starting something new."* GQ. https://www.gq.com.au/entertainment/music/bts-jin-interview/image-gallery/322978bb416f5e42d58e4e1743686176

7 Chin, C. (2022). *BTS' RM says having haters means the boyband are "in the mainstream"*. NME. https://www.nme.com/news/music/bts-rm-having-haters-means-boyband-in-the-meanstream-3204537

[8] Entertainment Tonight. (2021, Nov 22). *BTS on performing for THE ARMY in-person again (Exclusive)* [Video]. YouTube. https://www.youtube.com/watch?v=ZoZGv48u91Q

[9] The Late Late Show with James Corden. (2021, Nov 24). *BTS & Papa Mochi are reunited!* [Video]. YouTube. https://www.youtube.com/watch?v=pRl2tawentY

[10] BTS. (2020). UGH! [Song]. On *Map of the soul: 7*. Big Hit Entertainment.; Doolset. (2020, Feb 21). *욱 (UGH!)* [Translation]. https://doolsetbangtan.wordpress.com/2020/02/21/ugh/

[11] BTS. (2022). Run BTS [Song]. On *Proof*. Big Hit Entertainment.; Doolset. (2022, July 26). *달려라 방탄 (Run BTS)* [Translation]. https://doolsetbangtan.wordpress.com/2022/07/26/run-bts/

[12] Agust D. (2020). What do you think? [Song]. On *D-2*. Big Hit Entertainment.; Doolset. (2020, May 22). *어떻게 생각해? (What do you think?)* [Translation]. https://doolsetbangtan.wordpress.com/2020/05/22/what-do-you-think/

[13] Gregoire, S. W. (2020). *On an unbiblical view of suffering, wife abuse, and created to be his helpmeet*. To Love, Honor and Vacuum. https://tolovehonorandvacuum.com/2020/07/submission-debi-pearl-created-to-be-his-helpmeet-abuse/

[14] Jones, S. (2016). *An ATI education, final chapter: Guilty silence.* Recovering Grace. https://www.recoveringgrace.org/2016/01/an-ati-education-final-chapter-guilty-silence/

[15] Bailey, S. P. & Dueholm, B. J. (2015). *How purity invites fraud.* The Christian Century. https://www.christiancentury.org/blogs/archive/2015-09/how-purity-invites-fraud

[16] E! Insider (2017, Nov 18). *BTS boys reveal fans' weirdest requests and more! | E! Red Carpet & Award Shows* [Video]. YouTube. https://www.youtube.com/watch?v=j4QVVe5paHg

[17] Kang, D. (2017). *"The story of us coming up here from the bottom is our music itself"*. 조선일보. https://www.chosun.com/site/data/html_dir/2017/11/22/2017112202149.html?rsMobile=false

[18] Ko, J. (2021). *Anti-feminism website singled out celebs, lists RM from BTS as 'verified feminist'*. The Korea Herald. https://www.koreaherald.com/view.php?ud=20210813000594

[19] Pack, N. (2019). *3 times K-pop band BTS didn't care about playing it safe*. South China Morning Post. https://www.scmp.com/magazines/style/celebrity/article/3022621/3-times-k-pop-band-bts-didnt-care-about-playing-it-safe

[20] Byron, B.K. (2021). *BTS j-hope, global Army impressed with the release of dolls*. PRESSREELS. https://pressreels.com/bts-j-hope-global-army-impressed-with-the-release-of-dolls/9759

[21] (2019). *BTS's V caused this independent artist to completely sell out*. Koreaboo. . https://www.koreaboo.com/stories/bts-v-kate-rowland-paint-palette-pin-sold/

[22] Hussain, S. (2020). *Arcades - mots 7 interview*. BTS Radio UK. https://bts-radio-uk.blogspot.com/2020/05/arcades-mots-7-interview.html

[23] Chin, C. (2022). *Megan Thee Stallion says performing 'Butter' remix with BTS ive "Felt so good"*. NME. https://www.nme.com/news/music/megan-thee-stallion-says-performing-butter-remix-with-bts-live-felt-so-good-3152728

[24] (2019). *7 gentlemanly ways BTS have shown respect for women*. Koreaboo. https://www.koreaboo.com/lists/bts-women-respect-gentlemen/

[25] BTS. (2017). 21st century girl [Song]. On *You never walk alone*. Big Hit Entertainment.; Doolset. (2018, June 17). *21세기 소녀 (21st century girl)* [Translation]. https://doolsetbangtan.wordpress.com/2018/06/17/21st-century-girl/

[26] BTS. (2021). Butter [Song]. On *Butter*. Hybe.; Genius. (2021, May 21). *Butter* [Translation]. https://genius.com/Bts-butter-lyrics

[27] BTS. (2017). A supplementary story: You never walk alone [Song]. On *You never walk alone*. Big Hit Entertainment.; Doolset. (2018, June 17). *A supplementary story: You never walk alone* [Translation]. https://doolsetbangtan.wordpress.com/2018/06/01/a-supplementary-story-you-never-walk-alone/

[28] BTS. (2022). Yet to come (The most beautiful moment) [Song]. On *Proof*. Hybe.; Doolset. (2022, June 11). *Yet to come (The most beautiful moment)* [Translation]. https://doolsetbangtan.wordpress.com/2022/06/11/yet-to-come/

My soul's journey

Gardênia Pereira

TO UNDERSTAND A journey, it is necessary to know the starting point. My childhood is the central arc that reflects who I am today. As humans, our trajectory is rarely linear and it is common for us to travel unexpected routes, but there are certain things that do not change and certain circumstances that repeat themselves. I am Brazilian, 30 years old, and although I often present myself only as a psychologist, I am many others: writer, academic, ARMY. I try not to limit myself to just one identity. In order to analyse who I am and what I'm experiencing here and now, to properly show you my soul's journey, I find it important to contextualise my present experiences with my past. I've always heard from people around me that I was someone "difficult", but I was lucky to be understood by my parents. They saw me as a shy child, more observant than talkative, and who kept small circles of relationships. The starting point of my journey may have been in my childhood, in the search for a place where I find the freedom to be who I really am.

When I think of journeys and trajectories, automatically, stages or even metamorphoses come to my mind. Life is not linear, but cyclical after all. I have come to accept that there will be moments or stages that will not be so pleasant to relive or analyse, understanding this is essential to move forward. Freud proposes that, regardless of our desires, our condition as a human being imposes on us three sufferings: "that of having to deal with the superior power of nature; having to deal with the fragility of our bodies; and that of having to accept what civilization imposes on us, in order to adjust to the norms of a life in society".[1] This explains the inevitable suffering that I felt when I became an adult woman who couldn't find a place where I could have the freedom to be who I was: impose my limits, show things I like without fear of judgment, show my feelings. Freud presents two concepts to avoid such suffering in search of happiness. The first is likely to be achieved through stillness, that is, moving away from the outside world and seeking answers internally.[1] The second states that these answers are found when we become active members of a community, along with the help of psychotherapy, both which see us being open to new paths for change.[1]

When we think about our childhoods, for example, we can see that each of us can develop certain beliefs about ourselves, about other people, and about the world. These are called central beliefs, which are deep conceptions that people generally do not question and tend to take as absolute truths.[2] Therefore, these beliefs become limiting, because the thought can be so rooted that the person cannot think or act differently from what they believe to be right, which can cause dysfunctional and erroneous thoughts. Consequently, beliefs can cause significant discomfort for the person who has them, restricting them in numerous situations. In this context, because I was often silenced and excluded by certain groups, I developed beliefs that made me feel that I would have to adapt to a certain space, surpassing my individual preferences in order to fit into a pattern created by other people. Especially at school, where I had to agree with my peers even when I didn't want to, simply to be accepted by them. I don't know why my different opinions were a problem for them, but I always found myself making choices that pleased them first.

We act according to our beliefs. For me, understanding who I really was often prevented me from really liking who I had become. Self-love in theory is self-esteem. It is the acceptance of qualities, defects, achievements, failures, choices, and life experiences in their fullness. However, in practice it is difficult to measure what this actually means, knowing that each person understands, assimilates, and acts differently. I believe that I can only love myself when I truly know and accept who I really am.

In my case, being a psychologist made me who I am today, and marked the beginning of a new identity being formed, because seeing myself as being useful to the world has always been something I wanted. Psychology, through its abundant approaches, explains many phenomena such as patterns, behaviours, and coping mechanisms. It explains that as much as you think you are a complete person, who has already found your place, there is always room for progress and growth, as there will always be a lack, and we need to deal with this complexity. As much as, for me, psychology represented a 'place', there was another gap within me which was not yet filled. Something was missing that I didn't know... yet. In 2020, three years after I graduated from university, I still had not found the answer I was looking for and that was what prevented me from loving myself genuinely: 'Who am I?'

I usually associate changes with the seasons of the year, as both refer to cycles. When a season changes, everything around it changes too. The leaves that fall give way to dry branches that, with the rain, form new sprouts that allow the flowers to finally bloom. It may sound philosophical, but as one season turns into another, I feel like something in me changes along with it. My encounter with BTS in 2019 was the beginning of a new season in my life. It was during the release of their album *Map of the Soul: Persona* that the group caught my attention and became a new season for me. This new universe has provided me with many things: It transformed me as a person, it brought incomparable connections, both with BTS and with the friendships I have built as part of the ARMY fandom, and it showed me a new meaning of entertainment. Finding BTS gave me the strength I needed to accept myself as who I am and to free myself from many ties and barriers that I created.

The obstacles and questions that permeate our existence are inherent to human beings; we manage to avoid some, while others hurt us and leave scars. The first challenge when I became an ARMY was my age and finding BTS later on in their career. I always liked different musicians and bands, but I never experienced something like the 'BTS effect' before. It was the first time I got involved in a more intense way with an artist. Usually, people expect this intensity coming from teenagers and not from adult women. This is an immense prejudice, which I experienced through certain looks or questions from people in my life when I talked about my passion for BTS. At the time, at the age of 27, I started to question myself and even avoid talking about BTS with the people close to me. I was afraid that the fandom itself would not accept me because of my age.

Feeling the need to justify myself to certain people about BTS occupying a significant part of my life and that my feeling for the group was not just a phase was also something that bothered me. I believe that reducing this encounter to something fleeting is a big mistake. I was forever positively changed by BTS, being an ARMY was by no means fleeting.

It's time to bloom

In early 2020, I experienced a situation that destabilised me. Everything I had planned for my life suddenly has gone with the inexplicable ending of my seven-year relationship. I found myself without prospects or plans for the future. I was focused on a new chapter of my life that was about to begin: getting married, leaving my parents' house, building a new family. Suddenly, I had to let go of all the plans I had created, including abandoning feelings that had been watered down in my heart for many years. In a way, it reinforced my belief of not being deserving of love and acceptance by someone else.

In human development studies, Papalia, Olds and Feldman say that personality differences influence how people respond to life's events.[3] For example, a resilient person tends to experience an easier transition to certain situations in adulthood. At first, I repeated a pattern of behaviour—introspection. Due to the pandemic, I had plenty of time to reflect. During this period, I created a barrier and used a 'mask' that made everything appear well on the outside, while internally, I was in chaos. I chose to throw myself into work, and say yes to any proposal or opportunity that came up. My goal was to fill whatever time

I had so that I couldn't really think about the pain I was feeling, of not being loved, of not knowing what my mistake had been, if there was one. Due to my own unmet expectations, I felt lost. I questioned who I was, my confidence and my self-love. That's why I decided to focus on something that was not so destabilised, my professional life.

In our society, work plays an important role in our lives, and it is almost always this task that enables us to have many experiences, including exercising our ability to deal with problems and learn from our own unique journeys.[3] In mid-March, I received an invitation to help compose a project for academic ARMY. I put all the energy that was left in me into that project, and through this, changed my professional trajectory forever.

From the moment I joined two areas in my life, being a fan and being a researcher, a new reality opened up. I was able to meet new ARMY from around the world who were doing the same things as me. However, a new question arose: can I be both fan and academic? In the book *Fan Cultures*, Hills addresses the fan universe and the theories about them.[4] In it, the author emphasises the singularities of being an academic. He points out that academics are not completely rational, nor are fans absolutely immersed in their world. He adds that academic knowledge is not always significantly "testable", as well as fan knowledge is not always "informal" or "experiential".[4] As a result, we need to take into account the totality of the individual, as the experience of being a fan is part of a whole, of the unique experience of each of us, as well as the academic experience.

For a while, I heard that I should focus my efforts on working and making money with something that 'gave me a future' instead of wasting time being a fan. Hills states that the subjectivities embodied by fans or academics are, in most cases, concepts imposed on them.[4] And for that reason, many of us academic fans may not feel accepted within the academy.[4] Being part of a fandom that encourages education, culture, and promotes charity–which in mere days, or hours, raises significant amounts for various campaigns (Black Lives Matter[5] ; Fires in the Amazon[6] etc.)--makes me believe that we can break any barrier that annuls our experience and authenticity. I wondered over and over whether being part of a fandom would hurt my experience as a therapist and my adulthood. I internalised this questioning in a way and it was difficult to accept that I could be both and do them perfectly well, especially during a time when I found myself totally vulnerable. At that moment, being a psychologist and ARMY was part of my identity and spurred me forth on my journey in search of freedom to be who I chose to be.

I never walk alone

Believing in my potential and using my voice was the most genuine way I found to show the love and respect I have for myself and my story. Brené Brown, in the book *The courage to be imperfect*, says that loving yourself has to do with living fully, cultivating attitudes of courage and compassion towards your value and your "imperfections".[7] For me, loving myself also means identifying my limits so that I can recognise when I should ask for help, be it professionally or within my friend groups. I remind myself constantly to respect my processes and choices, to accept my vulnerabilities and complexities, in order to allow me to live the most diverse experiences possible.

Psychoanalytics proposes that every human being has three basic needs: the need to feel supported and safe; to feel accepted and valued; and, to belong.[1] When we speak for ourselves, the people who identify with who we are and the stories we tell eventually grow closer. The creation of bonds within the fandom was a very pleasant surprise. I was able to share my feelings with other people who were going through the same thing. I was able to explore the possibility of being both ARMY and an academic. *And that connection is powerful.* I feel that I belong somewhere, to a nucleus, to a group. And most amazing of all: I'm not afraid or ashamed to show it to people.

Being connected with ARMY and BTS makes me sure that even though life can hurt me in certain situations and make me tired, I must not give up, because in my heart I know that I am not alone. The Acceptance and Commitment Therapy (ACT) proposes a psychological flexibility, because, when inflexibility occurs, the individual demonstrates inertial behaviours, impulsivity, besides being stuck in harmful thought patterns.[8] It was necessary for me to accept my vulnerabilities and be willing to expose wounds in therapy to understand my harmful patterns and try to alleviate them. Acceptance was my greatest lesson.

The *Love Yourself* trilogy is the perfect example of how much ARMY is inspired and influenced by BTS. The speech made by RM at the UN in 2018 was the flame that was missing for me to start accepting and loving myself truly, and moreover: *acting*. I felt my heart sink when he said that he kept his voice to himself, and that he was just trying to fit into molds created by other people.[9] I realised that, like him, no matter how many flaws I have or how many mistakes I make, I will still be me. RM has music as a refuge and BTS became mine. RM helped me recognise that my voice matters and I need to speak for myself, because no one else will.

ACT asks us to accept the moment, and experience what we feel in its entirety, to increase actions that are based on values.[8] Accepting all the turmoil and experiencing it was in fact the way out that I needed to find. With the release of BTS' fifth studio album, *BE*, a new era arrived, filled with comfort and company messages, showing us that the journey continues, even in a time as turbulent as the pandemic. Like mine, the group's plans changed, they found themselves trapped in a really far away reality from the one they lived in before. Alone, away from the stages and the fans they love so much, they managed to reinvent themselves. With BTS as company, I made new and different paths: in addition to work as an academic ARMY (producing content and inspiring other researchers), I started a postgraduate course in neuropsychology, having in mind the relationship of people with music.

ACT also proposes to increase the capacity for change and "rescue" things that are pleasurable and make people feel better and consequently happier.[10] Certainly focusing on work and studies was the way I sought to achieve emotional balance, yet this process takes time and is something I still put my efforts into. Seeking professional, medical, and psychological help was extremely important to reaffirm what I believe about recognising and not exceeding my limits. There is a popular phrase that says 'the only way out is through', so we can only get out of a difficult experience by going directly through it. Currently, I am going through my adversities and strengthening my love for myself with the pillars that I believe support me: taking care of my physical and mental health, strengthening ties with my friends, and sharing love for BTS and ARMY.

Development theory states that young adults go through a time of profound changes in personal relationships in which people establish, negotiate, or consolidate bonds based on friendship, sexuality, and love. We take responsibility for ourselves and exercise our right to make our own decisions, in that sense friendships or passions can become lifelong bonds or disappear.[3] My connection with BTS, just like the rest of ARMY, is powerful. They are not only seven when they are with us, so I am not alone being part of ARMY. I intend to continue investing in self-care with the certainty that we are together on this journey amid bullets and obstacles, sailing and discovering ourselves in our own galaxy. As well as external changes, I know that internally we are liable to change all the time. And because of that, I know that my journey is long, so I will continue to nourish my soul with freedom and purpose.

References

[1] Freud, S. (1974). *O mal-estar na civilização. In o futuro de uma ilusão, o mal-estar na civilização e outros trabalhos* (Sigmund Freud's Brazilian standard edition of Complete Psychological Works), Vol. XXI. Rio de Janeiro: Imago.

[2] Beck, J. S et al. (2013). *Terapia cognitivo-comportamental: teoria e prática.* 2.ed. Porto Alegre: Artes Médicas.

[3] Papalia, D. E., Olds, S. W., & Feldman, R. D. (2006). *Desenvolvimento humano.* Porto Alegre: Artmed.

[4] Hills, M. (2002). *Fan cultures.* Psychology Press.

[5] Kwon, J.; Han, S. & France, L.R. (2020). *BTS e fãs doam mais de US$ 2 milhões para o movimento Black Lives Matter.* https://www.cnnbrasil.com.br/entretenimento/2020/06/08/bts-e-fas-doam-mais-de-us-2-milhoes-para-o-movimento-black-lives-matters

[6] Riveira, C. (2020). *Fãs de BTS arrecadam mais de R$ 37 mil em vaquinha para salvar o Pantanal.* https://exame.com/brasil/fas-de-bts-arrecadam-mais-de-r-37-mil-em-vaquinha-para-salvar-o-pantanal/.

[7] Brown, B. (2016). *A coragem de ser imperfeito.* Sextante: Rio de Janeiro.

[8] Hayes, S. C.; Pistorello, J.; Biglan, A. (2008). *Terapia de Aceitação e Compromisso: modelo, dados e extensão para a prevenção do suicídio.* Rev. bras. ter. comport. cogn., São Paulo , v. 10. http://pepsic.bvsalud.org/scielo.php?script=sci_arttext&pid=S1517-55452008000100008&lng=pt&nrm=iso.

[9] UNICEF. (2018). *BTS speech at the United Nations/ UNICEF* [Video]. YouTube. https://www.youtube.com/watch?v=oTe4f-bBEKg&t=3s&ab_channel=UNICEF.

[10] Cardoso, R.L. (2011). *Psicoterapias comportamentais no tratamento da depressão.* Psicol. Argum., Curitiba, v. 29, n. 67. https://periodicos.pucpr.br/index.php/psicologiaargumento/article/download/20359/19627.

Exiting the maze to find a spring day

Bianca Cuatico

THE JOURNEY TO becoming an ARMY starts with that fateful moment you encounter these seven incredible men. BTS. A saying exists within the fandom that you find BTS when you need them most. It seems like destiny or the universe had its hand in bringing them into our lives, with us not knowing how they would profoundly change us. I'm no different in this matter. In this chapter, I wanted to share my journey to being an ARMY, and why I have chosen to remain an ARMY. However, before we can get to that, I wanted to share how I was before finding BTS and ARMY.

Prior to life with BTS and ARMY, I was lost. I wasn't sure what I wanted and who I was. I was just going with the flow as I understood that decisions made for me were for my best interest. However as I got older, I began to question what it was I wanted. As time went on, my self-questioning of who I was got harder to ignore. It took discovering these seven men from South Korea and their music to help me discover who I am and be the best version of myself.

I have always been the "good girl". Always following the rules, obeying those older than me, and being by the book about things. This may be a big reason as to why, for a long time, it would matter what other people thought of me or whether my actions would affect others and how they viewed me. This didn't bother me when I was a teenager, or at least I wasn't really aware of these feelings until I was around 22. By then I felt suffocated.

There were only a few things I could remember being my choice, school clubs or organisations being the most prominent of them. High school electives, universities to apply for, degrees to take, the type of work I should do were all decided for me by my parents. I guess, subconsciously, that was why I loved my organisations and my best memories were there. I remember feeling like my school organisations meant everything to me back then and that they were my happy place. When I was in elementary and high school, I did artistic gymnastics. While in university, however, the organisation that meant the most to me was my university radio. Back then, I felt it was really all I had to look forward to.

After I graduated from university in 2014, I was pushed by my parents to start looking for a job right away, even though I had a scheduled trip to Europe within the next 4 months. It's traditionally expected in my country, the Philippines, that as soon as you graduate from college or university you have to immediately (if not having started prior to graduation) look for a job. Being a good daughter, I honoured their wishes and tried looking for work. Eventually, I was able to land a job after I returned from my trip. Even during the application period, however, what to apply for was being dictated to me.

Fast forward to 2017 and I can say I was at a low point in my life. I was in a dark place mentally and emotionally. I was anxious all the time. My mind could not settle down as I worried about every decision and action I made. I felt like I was walking on eggshells, always on edge, conforming to the image others projected onto me and the pressure I felt to live up to that. I felt lost and honestly didn't know what to do. You could say that things piled up through the years and that in 2017, I was close to the edge of breaking. I felt like I could not say what was on my mind and how I was feeling, scared that I would not be heard, and if I was heard, I might disappoint those I love. I felt trapped, like I was a bird in a cage. I was restless.

As time went by, I lost myself more and more. It terrified me and made me panic. At that point, I didn't know if my decisions were really mine or what others wanted for me. I had to reflect and think 'is this what I want?', and 'is this what is expected of me?' Not being able to distinguish between what it was I wanted and what others wanted for me made me question who I was and what it meant to be 'me'. Whenever I thought of that, I could not come up with an answer. A specific example would be when I was working in a headhunting company in 2017. I was incredibly unhappy with the work and company but when I would reflect on whether I really wanted this job and career path, I could not really say so since by then it would be close to three years doing this type of work. I didn't know anything else. At that point, I had discovered my love of writing. I had written some articles for my current and previous workplaces and found such joy in it. It was common knowledge that anyone moving out of the field of recruitment to a different career would have a hard time. I felt the need to set my love of writing aside and follow what was expected of me.

One night after work I opened my laptop, looking for something that could keep my mind off what I was feeling. For some reason, a video suggestion came up on my YouTube feed. It was a music video called *Mic Drop (Steve Aoki Remix)* by BTS, a Korean group that I had never heard of before. I don't know what it was that made me decide to click on the thumbnail, but I was not prepared for what I saw. Synchronised and complex choreography, on-point outfits, flawless transitions and effects, and savage yet classy lyrics. I remember rewatching the music video a few more times that evening. This piqued my curiosity since I had that feeling that they were different. I didn't exactly know why they were different at that time, but I wanted to see more. This was my first time with BTS, and I didn't know at that time that I was in for a hell of a wonderful ride.

After watching the *Mic Drop (Steve Aoki Remix)* music video, I wanted to see more content by these seven men. I decided to see what other music videos they had and the first one that came out on YouTube was a music video called *Spring Day*. The title made me curious about how this could relate to the thumbnail of a guy seeming to look up at something. On the first watch, I didn't turn on the English captions. I wanted to appreciate the visuals of the video, and I was not disappointed. I was captivated by the cinematography of the whole video. Every scene was picture-perfect, every colour scheme looked like a filter on Instagram. Even though I did not understand what they were saying, it was amazing how I could still hear and feel the emotions they wanted to express. On the second viewing, I turned the captions on as I wanted to see what the lyrics said. The first line, "I miss you. Saying this makes me miss you even more",[1] for some reason, that one simple line resonated with me. It was at that moment I had the sudden realisation that I didn't even notice how I had changed in a way that I had lost self-confidence compared to who I used to be. I was missing that part of me. You could say that I was hooked lyrically from that first line, as I felt so much truth in it. There was one line in particular in the song that struck me most and has been ingrained in me since I first read them. This one line that changed everything for me was, "The morning will come again. No darkness, no season can last forever."[1] Upon reading that line, I felt an immense sense of relief and comfort. Like I was being told whatever problems and concerns I'm facing right now, it will surely pass. It felt like a promise and that there was hope.

Spring Day, as explained by RM and Suga, is a song inspired by their own experiences about losing a friend, and by Jin as being about a sad event and about longing.[2,3] A popular theory video made by a fan shows the lyrics and music video being a tribute to the victims of the Sewol Ferry tragedy as well as their families.[4] Before learning about the theory and the event linked to it, the first time I heard the song and read the lyrics I had a different take on it. I saw it as me speaking to my old self. The lost and anxious me speaking to the younger, confident, and sure of herself version. It somehow felt like I was saying I missed the old me. I wondered how long it would be before I could be like that again, confident and self-assured. The lyrics comforted me by saying that the state I was in was not permanent and that I would be able to see the version of myself that I missed again. In all honesty, this is the song that made me an ARMY. For someone who values lyrics and the message they hold, it was possibly the first time in a long while since I heard and read such reflective words, and it had come right as I needed it most.

The era that I really started paying attention to BTS was during the *Love Yourself* era. This is the era that means the most to me, and I believe many ARMY would say the same. The story arc of the *Love Yourself* trilogy is something I consider to be a work of art and something many people can relate to. BTS' music helped me start discovering who I am and what it was I wanted. It was the start of self-discovery and self-acceptance.

Within these three albums, there is one song that solidified me being an ARMY for life. This was *Answer: Love Myself*. Suga's verse had particularly hit home for me when he said, "Perhaps, than loving someone else, it is more difficult to love myself. Let's be honest and admit what we have to admit that your standards are more strict when they are applied to you".[5] It was something I felt like I knew deep down but didn't acknowledge. So hearing that being laid out, along with the rest of the lyrics of the song, was such a relief and comfort to me. It felt like I was being told I'll be okay, I can walk the path I wish to go down, and that loving and knowing myself is an ongoing journey that I don't have to figure it out right away.

Once I knew I was in this BTS rabbit hole for life, I became more aware of the people who have been walking side by side next to the group, ARMY. It's remarkable how many people from different countries have been moved by these seven men to the point that they would take action in helping one another and making the world a better place. From organising charity projects, standing up for injustices again and again, and spreading the message of the band through events. It is shown that the small amounts contributed by individual people can create a significant impact if we work together. I found it incredibly unique how people, who are from different ways of life and nations around the globe, that don't even know one another personally, would band together to make a positive difference.

In the Philippines, there was one joint ARMY project that I was immensely proud to be part of even in a small way. In November of 2020, the Philippines was hit by a Category 4 typhoon called Ulysses (known internationally as Typhoon Vamco) which brought about the country's worst flooding since 2009. At least 180,000 people were evacuated, and in one city alone 40,000 homes were submerged.[6,7] Different ARMY fan bases throughout the country banded together to rally contributions to donate to affected families and communities. The fanbases worked with different local shops to get official and unofficial merchandise to raffle as a bonus for their contribution, and also set up different bank accounts that they could transfer funds to. The funds collected were used to gather food and essentials packs, and were donated to affected communities. During this time, I encouraged family members to help by having our household donate clothes to the people affected directly through our local community donation collection. Supporting different ARMY fanbases locally by making cash donations was also another small way I could help affected people. By November 20, the collective amount that ARMY in the Philippines was able to raise was over PHP 4 Million (USD 83,000).[8]

Being ARMY has helped me be kinder and give back to others. I support varying charity projects, animal sanctuaries, and often donate cash, books, food, medicine, clothing, and toiletries.

In the company where I work, we have a unique salary increase system where employees are not only evaluated on their work performance, but also on their passion (what they love and how it develops them) and their purpose (how they help and give back to society). In September 2020, after two years in the company, I decided to apply for this as I wanted to share my passion and purpose. I had decided to share being an ARMY as my passion and how being one affected me in my purpose of giving back through charity. I was worried that my presentation would not do justice to how being an ARMY has affected me and others. I wanted to show how being ARMY has helped shape people into being better versions of themselves, often resulting in them helping the world around them. After my presentation and the deliberation, I was fortunately told that my presentation was so well received that no further questions or evaluations needed to be done. The panel members gave me full marks on the salary increase, which was not easily given to people as there were limited places for it.

I never thought an artist or their songs could have such a profound impact on who I am. From being someone who was lost and could not even answer what it meant to be 'me' to the person who I am today who has not only started to learn who I am (and is still in this journey of self-discovery) but also someone who has begun to love myself as time goes by. The impact that BTS had on me not only affected me but has also affected how I view and treat the people around me in such a way that I have become a more empathetic and compassionate person. I remember having said to one of my ARMY friends last year that, though I have yet to experience romantic love, I never thought I would love someone so unconditionally as I do BTS. Where their wellbeing, happiness, and wanting the best for them was so important to me. As I write this chapter, I cannot help but be in tears as I recall all the emotions I have felt about how BTS have impacted me and what they mean to me. Being an ARMY has helped me be a better version of myself. Learning about and loving BTS has been the best decision of my life, and it all started when the universe decided, at the moment I didn't know I needed them most, that I should find them.

References

[1] BTS (2017). Spring day [Song]. On *You never walk alone*. Big Hit Music.

[2] Koreaboo. (2020). *Suga And RM discuss the inspiration behind BTS's mega-hit song "Spring day"*. https://www.koreaboo.com/news/bts-rm-suga-reveal-inspiration-behind-mega-hit-song-spring-day/

[3] Holmes, D. (2020). *The boundless optimism of BTS*. Esquire. https://www.esquire.com/entertainment/music/amp34654383/bts-members-be-album-interview-2020/

[4] bulletproof vibes. (2017, Feb 22). *BTS Spring Day MV EXPLAINED | Sewol ferry, snowpiercer & survivors* [Video]. YouTube. https://www.youtube.com/watch?v=Tye1ONFeKis

[5] BTS (2018). Answer: Love myself [Song]. On *LOVE YOURSELF 結 'Answer'*. Big Hit Music.

https://doolsetbangtan.wordpress.com/2018/08/24/answer-love-myself/

[6] Kottasová, I. & Sidhu, S. (2020). *Several killed and 180,000 evacuated as Typhoon Vamco hits the Philippines.* CNN. https://edition.cnn.com/2020/11/12/asia/typhoon-vamco-philippines-intl/index.html

[7] Reuters. *Typhoon Ulysses triggers worst floods in Metro Manila in years* (2020). Inquirer.Net. https://newsinfo.inquirer.net/1359823/typhoon-ulysses-triggers-worst-floods-in-metro-manila-in-years

[8] Tubiera, A. (2020). *When BTS members donate to charity they inspire fans to do the same – the 'Army' raised US$1 million for Black Lives Matter and US$83,000 for Typhoon Vamco victims.* https://www.scmp.com/magazines/style/celebrity/article/3113575/when-bts-members-donate-charity-they-inspire-fans-do-same

Fourteen hours

Emily Dunham

I WANTED TO CHANGE my name to Sarah when I was younger. It was what I called all my favourite toys—the blonde, plastic figurine with the mauve dress, the spotted rainbow pony, the stylish doll with soft, brown hair. I was certain that name would make me the type of girl I wanted to be–intelligent, charismatic, easily loved. It wasn't necessarily a lack of these characteristics on my behalf, but rather the perception that they would be amplified by being Sarah.

I asked my parents why Emily was the name they chose. My mom assured me the name hadn't gained its trendy factor when I was born in 1995, though its popularity did begin around that time. Sarah was also on their list of finalists, but something about Emily just stuck.

As luck would have it, I didn't mind being one of the Emilys.

I loved it.

A pivotal facet of my youth was being one of many. There was always someone else with my name. Even if we shared little else in common, we had the experience of existing as Emily. Being a part of something in such a fixed manner was important for a quiet child like me; it allowed me to both explore myself as part of a group and identify what made me different from said group. I was never completely alone, and what was more, I was always distinguished from the others in some way.

In third grade, I was the Emily who excelled at Connect Four.

In sixth grade, I was the Emily who could read 500 pages in a single Saturday afternoon.

In my sophomore year of high school, I was the Emily who played second chair clarinet in the marching band.

In college, I was the Emily who had a bartending job but rarely went out to bars.

As an adult, I find that I am more often the only Emily in a room, and the need for a specific distinction has diminished. My identity is more permanently intertwined between the letters, a soft ivy vine decorating the edges of each space. I have been given this name, but I have chosen what it will mean for myself, and what it will evoke when spoken regarding me.

Recently, one of the evocations has become being an ARMY. It seems like more than coincidence that the simple desire to learn the names of seven men led me here. It's something we all say to each other as a joke: "I just wanted to learn their names". But we are a species that places so much value in naming; perhaps it makes sense that this is the root of our curiosity.

Calling myself ARMY means many things to me, but at the core, it is a sort of renaming. We hope that when the members think of our name, it brings them solace. When I hear the members' names, I think of how each of the seven has taught me what it means to love all the pieces that make up my identity. Not as Sarah, or who I once wished I could be, but as Emily—who I am and who I will become.

RM: "We all have galaxies in our hearts."[1]

In the first few months of the COVID-19 pandemic, I felt motivated to fill the spaces left by social contact with productivity. My job at the animal shelter slowed down as our community stepped up to foster and adopt. I went for long walks around my neighbourhood, listening to podcasts. I attempted a yoga series and made a bullet journal. I read almost every book I owned. I made banana bread. I relished in the lack of social pressure.

However, after nearly ten months, I started to burn out on constant solitude. I had not seen my family or friends in almost a year. I was just getting through the days at work. I lost the energy for yoga and baking. I ran out of ideas for journaling. I felt each ounce of motivation and passion slowly leaving me.

Shortly after Thanksgiving 2020, a friend told me she was hooked on the song *Dynamite* by BTS and sent me their Carpool Karaoke video. 16 minutes and 49 seconds–that's all it took to change my life. One video became ten as I scoured YouTube for more interviews with the band. I was magnetised by their effortless humor, their confidence, and their undiluted talent. However, what struck me most in the beginning was the way they always expressed genuine gratitude to ARMY, regardless of their accomplishments. I watched Carpool Karaoke again, trying to pick a bias and failing. I saved their Spotify playlist. As I walked the dogs through the wooded path at work, sometimes I'd play them a song or two.

For me, BTS was initially something that could fill the vacant spaces created by a worldwide pandemic. They felt like friends and family in a time that we could not be with our own. While there were no mimosas for Christmas brunch or Scattergories with my family, I did start learning Hangul. I couldn't visit the local library, but I still read books that RM recommended. I couldn't go to the gym any more, but I could listen to BTS during my weekly outdoor run.

In 2017, RM changed his stage name from Rap Monster to RM. He explained the name had "become different from [what I want] to put at the front of the music I've made for the past five years, and the music I want to share in the future".[2] Perhaps his original stage name sounded formidable at a younger age, but as he got older, it wasn't representative of who he was becoming. The acronym no longer stands for one specific thing; it is ever-changing. Becoming ARMY feels like that; like the ability to rename and reinvent yourself, especially in the face of uncertainty. Similar to RM, I once wanted my name to be connected to phrases I deemed impressive, such as being a tennis co-captain or maintaining perfect attendance at school. As an adult, I'd like it to represent larger core sentiments: authenticity, gratitude, and strength.

Jin: Feminist ARMY

There is a duality in being a woman. I am soft and strong, courageous and kind. I can find infinite ways to redefine femininity. Even so, tendrils of sexism are constantly lurking in my life. I want to be described as more than hair and eyes and hips. I want to be the hand to hold in the quiet of loss, the voice to hear when thinking of home. I want to be perceived as the best version of myself, but this is a version that ebbs and flows. To fully embrace this self, I must also struggle against what society expects of me.

As the member most often referred to as a visual or Worldwide Handsome, I think Jin perfectly encapsulates what it means to be seen as a collection of physical traits, rather than as a whole person. In most American interviews, his handsomeness is the central talking point (if he is spoken to at all). The characteristics that ARMY loves—his corny humour or his impressive vocal range, his passion for cooking or his ability to lift the mood of a room—are most often highlighted in content produced by their label. However, Jin has turned his beauty into something more powerful, something that acts as a mere prologue to who he really is. It may be the enticing factor for new fans, but his warmth and self-confidence are why people stay. This, beyond anything else, is how he has inspired me to love each layer of myself.

When I began to show an interest in K-pop, I noticed that many people were dismissive of the genre. As with any sort of media traditionally perceived as feminine, BTS is subject to "derisive discourse", especially when it comes to their fanbase.[3] Though ARMY is not entirely female (over 45,000 surveyed fans last year identified as male or non-binary),[4] we are certainly subject to misogyny. We are discounted as 'fangirls' or 'groupies' regardless of demographic data showing otherwise.[3, 4] Unfortunately, this brand of invalidation is not novel to me. Despite having a degree in animal behaviour and years of experience in canine behaviour, training concepts are mansplained to me on a regular basis. In the gym, men approach me unbidden to explain machines that I have been using for years. It is difficult to be "women in a man's world, discounted because of a trait that goes to the core of who [you] are".[5] So though unsurprising, it was still disheartening to have BTS become yet another aspect of my life that was minimised.

Many might ask why I feel being ARMY has enhanced my feminism. While BTS is a male group, ARMY is a powerful, majority female fandom. BTS has inspired fans around the world to participate in various charities and social movements, as well as self-reflection and growth. If much of that positivity originates from women, it is just another example of female power. On an individual level, being ARMY has made me more cognizant of the stigma that is attached to so many supposedly 'female' interests. I was initially hesitant to embrace my curiosity about BTS due to this type of preconception, but now I am unapologetically ARMY. Gendering a music genre only perpetuates stereotypes and discourages people from engaging, which is something I no longer allow to happen to me. Women deserve to find joy in any space, regardless of public perception.

Alone, facing misogyny is insurmountable. Together, we can be agents of change. We are every embodiment imaginable of humans. We are united by love for music, healed by our unity, and inspired by our power. I can think of few words that summarise our bond better than Jin's: "In a world full of uncertainty, we must cherish the importance of "me", "you", and "us"".[6]

Suga: Shadows are followed by light

"... It's not about facing your shadow or fighting your shadow, but just acknowledging the fact you have your shadow". [7]

I spent a long time denying that I am an introvert. I was a social butterfly all through school; always at a choir rehearsal, a tennis match, or a movie night. Yet as I got older, I felt drained trying to keep up this level of social engagement. I yearned for the type of established, comfortable friendship portrayed between idol group members, but I also required some level of solitude to recuperate from the expended energy of a work week. I thought about Suga, an introvert who is both doted on by his members and allowed to retreat without question. How did he strike this balance? I was at war within myself, seeking an equilibrium that seemed impossible to reach.

It wasn't until I read *Quiet: The Power of Introverts in a World That Can't Stop Talking* by Susan Cain that I fully claimed the introvert label. Her distinction between 'shy' and 'introvert' particularly resonated with me. As Cain says, "Shyness is the fear of social disapproval or humiliation, while introversion is a preference for environments that are not overstimulating".[5] I am an introvert, but I am not shy. This was a revelation; it was something I knew, but had not yet been able to articulate. I am opinionated and creative, but I do not enjoy lengthy periods of social engagement without respite. My flat became my equivalent to Suga's studio, minus the "go away" doormat.[8]

My Midwestern upbringing shrouded a greater truth: though common, introversion is geographically concentrated in other places, with Asia being the most introverted and the U.S. being the most extroverted.[5] This too was revelatory for me. I can be mighty and quiet, accomplished and introspective. Perhaps this was the secret that allowed Suga to thrive in an industry that can require so much social energy. His quiet timbre and honest attitude regarding his social battery are some of his most beloved traits. He is surrounded by a culture that acknowledges and embraces his introversion.

It took me longer to reach this point of acceptance. Because it is uncommon in American media to see introverted traits celebrated, I spent many years subconsciously regarding the entire concept as negative. Conversely, Suga cemented only positive associations in my mind. From him, I've learned about establishing boundaries and routines, nurturing friendships that accept me, and choosing hobbies I can engage in alone or in small groups. He is certainly one of the members that I feel the strongest kinship with; his quiet caretaking, his love of words, and his comfort in solitude reflect pieces of myself. He makes me feel at home in a quality that I spent years believing I should change.

j-hope: "Inhale, inhale, exhale, exhale"[9]

I work with dogs in an animal shelter. Some are just unlucky; their owners have lost their homes, a landlord won't allow the breed, or money is tight. Some are injured or missing their fur. Many are reunited with relieved owners. Most will be adopted.

Ever since I started this job, I've believed that working with behaviourally challenging dogs requires a delicate balance of bravery and caution. Most dogs do not want to resort to biting, and if we communicate effectively with them, much of the risk is mitigated. I am proud of this work, especially when I look back at the numbers. In just over four years, I've worked with over six hundred dogs, and we have been able to place more than 90% of them.

During the pandemic, my work became my life. There was little else to focus on, and it seemed nearly impossible to step away. I felt buried beneath an avalanche of abandoned animals with no end in sight. I remember watching the *Dear Class of 2020* speech and j-hope said, "There will be times in your life when you question your own decisions...whether you are doing well or walking the path of failure."[10] I certainly questioned if this was the right path for me, there were so many days that I felt like I was failing. When we couldn't safely place a dog after months of work. When adoption applications fell through. When I took two jobs to make ends meet. I was following my passion, but how long can passion last in conjunction with stress and compassion fatigue?

It seemed as though the courage I had when facing the dogs was failing when it came to facing myself. I could look at a snarling dog and recognise the fear behind the teeth. I could identify when to maintain distance and when to finally open the kennel door. That's what clicked for me: Despite loving this work, I needed to maintain that barrier between the job and my life, or risk losing myself. I needed to allow myself an existence outside of being a dog person. Bravery did not entail marching endlessly towards burnout; it required me to face myself, fears and all.

j-hope recently released his first solo album, *Jack In The Box,* which explores darker concepts such as self-destruction and ambition. He has presented one side of himself for many years; sunshine, splashes of colour, and laughter. All of those aspects remain a part of him, but in his album promotions, he repeatedly emphasised a need to show other sides of himself in his art.[10] This was an act of vulnerability and bravery, and in my opinion, the result was his best work yet. *Jack In The Box* is more than just an album, though, it's an encouragement to anyone that has felt trapped within the walls of expectation. I had *MORE* on repeat for weeks in the car. It feels like a reminder that whether or not I work in animal welfare permanently, it is only one part of me. There will always be opportunities to explore my version of more, and hope will always remain.

Jimin: *I Need U*

Years ago, there was a personality quiz you could take and then share a link for others to reply about you. After meticulously considering my answers, I eagerly awaited responses. It was disappointing, then, to discover that my friends had given answers a world apart from mine. It was like being told that they didn't know me, or maybe worse: I didn't know myself.

I started to wonder about which version of me was a true representation, since there were clearly multiple Emilys floating around. I can imagine the responses would have varied further had my family or other peer groups also taken the quiz. This was all long before I had encountered the concept of persona, but years later, the idea certainly applies to my young life crisis. I realise now that wearing metaphorical masks is simply a part of being a social creature. I can accept that everyone will see their own version of me, and that my true self is an amalgamation of these.

As my comfort with this individuated self grew, I felt increasingly connected to the idea of independence. I sought to exist in such a way that I didn't need anyone; I saw dependence on others as weakness. A part of me believed that this was sustainable, but a deeper understanding of human nature would suggest otherwise. Regardless of my resistance, our species has a need for connection—we cannot thrive without it. In a 2018 video log, Jimin describes how that same internal resistance to leaning on others caused him to feel adrift and lonely. Reconnecting with his members and reminiscing on moments with ARMY was what reinvigorated him.[12, 13] In the same way, I have been drawn out of every dark moment in my life by some form of human connection, whether it be a call from a friend or a song by seven men across the world.

It's strange to think that people you've never met can provide such comfort. Yet when I replay episodes of *Run! BTS* or listen to *BE*, that is the strongest emotion I feel. The vulnerability and softness that we see in their content, especially from Jimin, encourages me to break from patterns of isolation. Simply put, engaging with BTS is egosyntonic for me. Perhaps the only lens that this connection makes sense through is that of the collective unconscious.[14] I am one ARMY Bomb in a sea of purple, a single voice in a fanchant chorus. We are all merely small pieces, drawn together by fate or chance, to form a whole. Despite our separate lives and ambitions, despite barriers of language and geography, ARMY grows. A closed microcosm rarely thrives, but together, we form the Mikrokosmos.

V: "Where's my angel?"[15]

"Every time when I'm thinking about something or have to make a decision, I picture this imaginary being, "Angel"." [16]

I wanted to write books when I was younger. I completed a binder of short stories by the time I was in high school, some of which were downright strange. I wrote about the SuperHearts, a coalition of heroes drawn as hearts with braids and faces. They liked to dine on tea and crumpets, though I had no idea what crumpets were. I wrote an entire series on a girl with especially stinky breath that was loosely based on an unkind classmate. I created a horror scene with human-sized yellow jackets at a school dance.

As I got older, I wrote poems to process heartbreak, loneliness, and death. I could hide the reality of my anxieties in imagery, drape my depression in a cloak of synonyms. I wrote about people I admired in hopes of showing them how poetic humans can be. I took the bodies of dogs I could not save and turned them into sonnets. I personified the honey locust tree as a femme fatale.

A piece of my identity is being a writer, though it is more of my shadow than my self. It is simply an instinct, a place I have been guided towards time and time again, even if there are times that I lack the right words or inspiration. I find solace in the practice, yet it is a part of me that I am often unwilling to share. I can reach a serenity in writing that is inaccessible in much of my life; language is my escape.

In part, I think this is why *Blue & Grey* is my favourite song. It's one of those rare tracks that elicit goose bumps on the first listen. For V, the song functioned as a way to handle burnout and depression.[17] The reference to his angel is particularly striking to me, because it echoes the force I feel while writing. This specific personification gives a name to a sensation that I have experienced my entire life, but never had words to describe.

It may be that we are looking within ourselves for answers, becoming our own guiding light without conscious recognition. Regardless, there is certainly an energy that inspires me to write, whether it is in a dilapidated sign on the side of the highway or the childhood characters that appeared in my mind's eye. Angels of some sort must be at play, humming a melody to a song or whispering a line into a poet's ear.

Jung Kook: Create your reflection

My body has always been a place of fluctuation. As a child, I was called chicken legs more times than I can count. As I grew older, my body became softer and I began a battle against it. For a time, I starved myself of nutrients; I was always cold, always hungry, always thinking about calories. I remember sitting in math class and eating a granola bar, so I could stop being dizzy long enough to focus. I would spend hours running or on the elliptical until I was nauseous. I considered a handful of crackers a meal. I played it all off under the façade of fitness.

I didn't truly love the gym until I started lifting weights at 19. Suddenly, I was gaining muscle and forgot about the number on the scale. Instead of looking for my ribs, I would admire the way my shoulders rounded out, my core strengthened, and my calves grew. I found group classes that challenged me and instructors who offered me guidance. I gave myself grace to miss the gym when my body needed rest. Seeing myself get stronger was empowering, and it still allowed me a sense of control in my body.

There have been innumerable people who have told me how I should be using my body, especially after I stopped trying to be skinny. I've heard that I should be doing more cardio, that I'll hurt myself using weights, that it's not feminine, that I should wear gloves to prevent calluses. Men have stopped me in the middle of sets to question my routine or tripped while staring at me. Yet I still feel at ease when I'm in the weight room. I'm creating the self that I want to see, not a version to appeal to someone else's gaze.

I love all the ways humans make our bodies feel like home. We can dye our hair or paint our nails, lift weights or take up a sport. Our bodies are the first home we will ever know and the only one we will never leave behind. Regardless of the number of times I tried to knock myself down, burn away the architecture of my being, reduce myself to rubble, my body remained. I have reconstructed my form, from the tattoos on my forearms to the seven hoops in my ears.

Jung Kook, too, has made his body his home. Though his tattoos may be controversial in South Korea, some believe that the surge of popularity in body art points to a larger shift towards individualism and challenging prejudice.[18] This denotes a key factor in contemplating our physicality, our bodies are not the reason we are loved. I'd like to imagine that the way we present ourselves is merely a projection of intangible characteristics we hope others will see. My muscles depict a deeper strength — my monochromatic style, a sense of practicality. In Jung Kook's tattoos, I see his patience and strong sense of self. In his voice, I hear his ardent desire to constantly improve. In short, it is our individuality and our passions that will attract others. As

Jung Kook demonstrates, our bodies simply provide the basic structure for our greater essence, and we are the architects.

ARMY: "We were the bullet, and you guys were the proof. So we're now truly bulletproof".[19]

Between Seoul and Indiana, there is a time difference of fourteen hours. It's more than half a day, the distance between dusk and dawn. Much of the time, when we are all home, I am living an entirely different day than any member of BTS. It may seem impossible to connect with anyone so far away. It may seem unlikely that we can understand each other at all when my Korean is limited to the four hundred words I've managed to memorise so far. ARMY is often belittled for our dedication to seven men that will rarely even occupy the same room as us. Many have deemed the parasocial relationship unhealthy. But take a look at all it has offered us, or even just me.

I am ARMY because RM invited me to be unafraid to redefine myself.
I am ARMY because Jin reminded me that together, we are powerful.
I am ARMY because Suga showed me how to embrace being an introvert.
I am ARMY because j-hope always has a smile to offer in the face of change.
I am ARMY because Jimin offers vulnerability even when it feels hard.
I am ARMY because V helped me believe in angels.

I am ARMY because Jung Kook encouraged me to build myself up.

When you divide fourteen hours in half, you have only seven. That feels like we aren't so far apart after all.

References

[1] Hiatt, B. (2021). *The triumph of BTS*. Rolling Stone. https://www.rollingstone.com/music/music-features/new-bts-song-2021-worlds-biggest-band-1166441/

[2] Herman, T. (2017). *BTS' rap monster changes stage name to RM*. Billboard. https://www.billboard.com/music/music-news/bts-rap-monster-rm-changes-stage-name-8031462/

[3] Gerrard, Y. (2021). *Groupies, fangirls and shippers: The endurance of a gender stereotype.* American Behavioral Scientist. https://doi.org/10.1177/00027642211042284

[4] Grover, C., Ciocirlea, R., & Santero, N. (2021). *Results*. BTS ARMY CENSUS. https://www.btsarmycensus.com/results

[5] Cain, S. (2013). *Quiet: The power of introverts in a world that can't stop talking*. Broadway Books.

[6] BANGTANTV. (2020, September 23). *BTS (방탄소년단) speech at the 75th UN General Assembly* [Video]. YouTube. https://youtu.be/5aPe9Uy10n4

[7] BANGTANTV. (2019, April 18). *BTS global press conference 'Map of the soul'* [Video]. YouTube. https://youtu.be/Tki_BNr8QtY

[8] 방탄소년단. [@BTS_twt]. (2018, March 8). *이 분의 생일 리액션이란..* #슈가생일ㅊㅋ [Tweet, attached video]. Twitter. https://twitter.com/BTS_twt/status/971763874700537856

[9] j-hope. (2022) MORE [Song]. On *Jack In The Box*. Big Hit Music.

[10] BANGTANTV. (2020, June 7). *BTS commencement speech: Dear class of 2020*. YouTube. https://youtu.be/AU6uF5sFtwA

[11] BANGTANTV. (2022, July 19). *j-hope 'Jack In The Box' album interview.* YouTube. https://youtu.be/umSGz3WtLMg

[12] SPOTLIGHTBTS. (2019, February 25). *[Eng sub] 180413 Jimin*. YouTube. https://youtu.be/pnfgDmrr730

[13] BANGTANTV. (2019, February 25). *180413 Jimin*. YouTube. https://youtu.be/X2kfDA_jqw0

[14] Jung, C. G. (1936). The concept of the collective unconscious. *Collected works, 9* (1), 42.

[15] BTS. (2020) Blue & Grey [Song]. On *BE*. Big Hit Music.

[16] BANGTANTV. (2021, February 28). *BTS (방탄소년단) V's BE-hind 'full' story*. YouTube.
https://youtu.be/4T6oiXKDPyI

[17] Kang, M. (2021). *V: "I have a desire to perfect one cool thing about myself"*. Weverse Magazine. https://magazine.weverse.io/article/view?lang=en&colca=1&num=212

[18] MacFarlane, Morgan. (2019). *Tattoos in East Asia: Conforming to individualism.* Sound Ideas.
https://soundideas.pugetsound.edu/asianstudiesstudents/4

[19] Kim, N. (2021). *Permission to dance on stage.* Los Angeles; SoFi Stadium.

My existence is impressive, unique, and important

Martyna Kučinskaitė

Generation of post-Soviet kids

GROWING UP IN Lithuania, a country that was just recovering from its last occupation, always felt like we were too small to have big dreams. We were too unimportant to share our opinion on global topics, and barely deserved to be alive or have the freedom that we fought for so strongly. There was still so much to be afraid of in late 1990s and early 2000s: A possibility to be occupied again by bigger and more powerful countries, to be declined from getting into the European Union and NATO, and to miserably fail once again and disappear from the map of the world for good. Lithuania, my motherland and such an old country, that once spread through Europe up to the Black Sea, over the years became a dwarf country with under three million citizens.

I was born six years after Lithuania restored its independence and finally freed itself from the Soviet Union. All my life I've been told by my parents that I can become whoever I want to be, but the sad reality of a recovering country throws a heavy shadow over those big dreams. When I was just two or three years old, I only wanted to be the lady behind the baked goods counter in a grocery store—I did not want to bake those cakes, but solely sell them to the people who would really want to eat them. At the age of three and a half, my parents started teaching me to play piano and saw great potential for me becoming a professional pianist one day. Even then, I still felt that I had a wide variety of choices of who I could become—a president, an astronaut, a lawyer, a banker. My little self was aiming for big roles which could impact the people around me and help my recovering country, make things better and life easier for everyone, including myself. I did not necessarily feel the calling for all those positions, but as long as they were powerful positions, I wanted to aim for them like the Moon and then maybe land somewhere on the stars. However, even with my parents' support, having such big goals at that time was not easy for anyone my age.

The generation of kids who were born after the 1990s experienced quite a lot of two-sided treatment from the elders. While they cherished us for being the kids of free Lithuania, we have never avoided comments about having it easier than our parents and grandparents. I remember being constantly shown photos and videos from the occupation years at school, told stories in my family about the mass deportations to Siberia, every year on the national memorial days hearing about the number of people that we lost on the news and especially the 14 heroes who died fighting for our freedom that one cold January night. I could never really escape the horrors that my people went through, and equally was made responsible to continue the work that country's most noble people started before me. When the whole country was mainly focusing on recovering economically and rebuilding cities, trying to find its own identity again and erase the labels that this occupation gave us, I never felt like there was the right time to start my own individual exploration and expression. My thoughts kept going in circles with questions such as 'How would this help my country?' or 'Will this lead me to a powerful position, where I could make kind-hearted decisions helping everyone around me?' All I felt that my homeland expected from me was to worship the heroes from the past days and continue to sacrifice myself for Lithuania, unless I wanted to be called an ungrateful and spoiled child.

Searching for someone to look up to

When I was a teenager, people started asking me who my role models were. Sadly, I've never had an answer to this question. It would have been best to say that I admire one of our great patriotic writers or priests from the past few decades, for they have been keeping everyone's spirits up during the most difficult times in my country's history. I could have chosen politicians, brave civilians, or even artists, who have been inspiring everyone to keep moving forward and creating, not expecting much gain for themselves while being the beacons of hope to others. Unfortunately, I did not feel that connection to any of them. I thought they were very brave and I respected every one of them, but I did not want to be like them. I started realising that my big dreams about becoming someone in power, who could help my motherland and people around me, were going to take away the freedom and personal joy from me. Dedicating oneself to bettering others most often comes at a price of drained energy and no personal time nor freedom of having individual dreams and aspirations. That is a real sacrifice which I aspired to when I was little, but no longer felt such calling. I did not want to become a hero any more.

At some point in my life, when I was very religious and still in high school, I tried to relate to the Christian saints who dedicated their lives to understanding God and getting closer to Him rather than serving for the physical world's constructions. It felt freeing for a few years to follow well-respected figures, and for some time I claimed that my role model was a Lithuanian Polish nun named Faustina Kowalska. To this day, I think that she is one of the most extraordinary saints that the Catholic Church has. Even living a very difficult life, she always fought for her truth to be heard.[1] I remember reading stories from her diary describing her persistence, believing in herself and fighting for the truth. All of these qualities that Fausitina had—courage, faith, strong will power, persistence, and absolute dedication to one's practice—resonated with me when I was following her steps. I admired her at that time, but I was not inspired, nor did I want to follow the same path as her.

After graduating high school, I chose to study music, piano performance. I was once again met with a lot of fanatic people, only this time they were admiring famous composers and performers to the point where they would try to imitate them to the last detail while performing the same pieces. I remember one of my friends being so into Rachmaninoff that he always carried a thick book about the composer and played piano pieces only by him whenever it was possible. I loved studying piano and exploring many genres and composers that I have not played before, but again, never felt such a strong connection that others did with at least one of the famous figures of the classical music world.

Four years later I graduated with a bachelor's degree, not having had a single real role model in my life yet. It felt like I was floating in space. It is one thing to not compare yourself to others and stop treating this life like a race, but it's another to have no one to look up to and slowly lose the sense of being important at all. Having a role model does not mean that I want to become an exact copy of them. It simply means having an example, knowing that what they did is possible, so I can do it too. I've been searching for such an authority figure my whole life and found it only at the age of 23, when I unexpectedly discovered BTS. It was the first time in forever when I truly felt such a close bond with someone and they became my role models, my true idols.

BTS finds you when you need them the most

There is a well-known saying amongst ARMY, that BTS finds you when you need them the most. It may sound like we think of BTS as some angelic saviours who are sent from the heavens by gods to heal the sad, the anxious, and depressed. From first sight BTS and ARMY may even look like a religious community that has its idols worshipped by people who seek for inner peace, happiness, and self-growth. The good thing about BTS is that to be comforted by them and ARMY there is no faith required or denied, no rules or practices mandatory, no worthy or unworthy people, only the strong sense of community, belonging, love, and joy (that could probably be even stronger—in my personal experience—than the most religious communities have today). Everyone chooses to be here of their free will and not because of the consequences if chosen differently. We are here simply because we enjoy talking to each other about the things we like, we can express emotions we experience freely, and share the ideas that are born along the way.

I found BTS, or BTS found me, two years ago, right before I started my second year of my master's degree in piano performance in New York City. I had just spent all summer of 2020 not being able to fly home to Lithuania to visit my family and friends due to the global pandemic. I stayed completely alone in one of the busiest cities in the world. Yet it felt so strange, because it was barely alive at this time. My college friends had left the city to go home to other states and I also could not meet the ones who stayed, because everyone was afraid of catching the virus. Even when hanging out with someone in a park there were no hugs, no friendly patting on the shoulder, or childishly holding hands while walking. I was alone with or without people around me, and felt lonelier than ever. I was trying my best to simply survive the summer and get back to studying and work as soon as possible.

That summer made me miss not only being able to touch my friends freely without a death threat, but also making music together–playing in ensembles, performing with an orchestra, singing in a choir, going to the concerts–all the things that I came to do in New York City were taken away from me. I felt betrayed and hopeless, I felt that it was just not fair to be going through such things. The pandemic was and still is extremely difficult for everyone, but from my personal perspective I can understand the best how all performers, BTS included, were feeling. No live concerts for me meant no real, strong emotions, no thrills, no overwhelming feeling of catharsis that I get leaving the stage after the performance, no communicating through music with other musicians and the audience, no hearing of the real-life applause... It was like one of my senses was taken away, as if I was made mute.

And then, one dull night of my endless binge-watching sessions on YouTube, I was watching a reaction video on Roomie Official's channel, where the host Joel was reacting to the new song by BTS called *Dynamite*. Up to that point in time I had never heard BTS' music, let alone anything K-pop related. (Later I discovered that I knew one song that featured BTS—it was *Waste It On Me* by Steve Aoki. I loved that song without knowing who BTS was and that a few members were singing on that record as featuring artists from the seven member group). The first time I heard *Dynamite*, it absolutely enchanted me from the first few seconds in. Right after Joel's reaction was over, I went to (then called) Big Hit Entertainment's official YouTube channel and watched the music video. And then I watched it again, and again, and again. I couldn't stop smiling! I think that night I watched *Dynamite* at least 20 times in a row and then proceeded to search for other people reacting to it and getting excited about everything all over again. I could not comprehend how an almost four-minute video was so well-made, kept my attention for all its length without any breaks, how each member was so different, charming, and funny, and how the whole experience was so engaging. I was fascinated by something so simple (from the first look), so well put together, edited, and executed to make me smile, laugh, and gasp watching it for the 20th, 30th, and 100th time. That was the day when I discovered

BTS and the moment when I realised that what BTS creates is not just a performance or putting up a show, they create an extraordinary experience for those who have an open heart and mind to receive it.

After *Dynamite*, I went to listen to a few more songs that were released by BTS earlier in 2020, like *Stay Gold*, *ON*, and *Black Swan*. I didn't jump into their over 300-song discography right away, I just rewatched the same few videos and then searched for people listening to those songs for the first time—just to experience that same excitement all over again, even if it's through someone else's eyes and ears. And then I dived deeper into the other side of BTS, which is what ARMY jokingly calls 'free therapy' or 'healing content'. I was learning their names and getting to know their personalities through interviews and funny moments videos that ARMY collects and releases on YouTube almost daily. I fully merged into the fandom, even with my classes going on during the day. Right when they were over, I would head to YouTube for my daily dose of BTS therapy. I knew I could be calm and trust that anything BTS related will make me feel better no matter what.

Chasing happiness is a good thing

A few months later their new album, *BE*, was released, and it was my first comeback as a pretty young ARMY at the time. The level of vulnerability these artists shared with millions of their fans impressed and inspired me. I started thinking that they are not only doing something right, but they are also doing everything right and that I have never seen anyone do it like them before.

Even when I was still struggling with my mental health all fall and winter, with BTS in my life, I felt like I had a life raft. They were the reason I spent my lonely hours of the day laughing instead of apathetically staring at the white, cracked ceiling of my rented room in an old Victorian house. They inspired me to go figure out why I'm so down and taught me that despite these sad emotions I'm experiencing now, I deserve all the happiness in the world.

BE was like a healing package and I loved all the comforting songs BTS created during this difficult time, but two tracks touched me the most—*Blue & Grey* and *Dis-ease*. *Blue & Grey*'s lyrics were so accurate to my current mental state that it scared me at first; V really described how I was feeling without even knowing me. It was amazing to have someone understand how I was feeling better than myself and put it into words and beautiful melodies while also bringing a message of comfort and hope that better days are coming. *Dis-ease* at first few listens was so strange and full of contrasting elements, blended genres, and unexpected changes of flow, but once I came to understand what was happening in it musically, it made me dance and want to be creative again. It became a song that could pull me out of the slump from one listen per day. Even now, every time I listen to *Dis-ease* it feels like j-hope's sunshine-like energy is oozing through that track and filling me with happiness and hope. It has become one of my all-time favourite songs by BTS to this day.

The following months were even more difficult to me, and I clung onto BTS harder than ever. The end of the fall semester was extremely challenging to juggle studies, work, and my crumbling mental health. In the mornings, I didn't feel like getting out of bed, because I was exhausted after only a few hours of sleep. I was spending most nights studying or not being able to fall asleep due to anxious thoughts endlessly running through my mind. When I had to go to the most important lectures in person, I would put BTS' *ON* on the highest volume that my headphones could handle and let the marching beat make my feet put one in front of another. After a long day, I would play *00:00 (Zero O'Clock)* and cry about how tired I am from this never-ending survival mode since the pandemic started. I have learned to let myself fully experience these heavy emotions and when the song was over, I would be left with a little bit of hope that would help me to keep going for the next couple hours until I break down again. *00:00 (Zero O'Clock)* lyrics "And you gonna be happy"[2] were the ones that I held onto the most. Right before the new year, I made a conscious decision to get better and started going to therapy with a very clear purpose—to feel happy again.

There were numerous times when BTS and their songs got mentioned during my therapy sessions. Once in cognitive behaviour therapy exercises, I was listing the people who I find inspiring, and I remember writing down Suga as someone who seems to have this amazing peace of mind, great work ethic (that I wish I had some day), and most importantly the courage to fight his inner demons with vulnerability sharing his own journey with the world. In the list of what makes me happy I would include entertaining BTS' content, such as the *RUN BTS* variety show, their VLives, old and new live performances in front of the huge crowds, and funny interviews. Then I realised that this obsession with BTS, especially when everything is still shiny and yet to be discovered being a very new fan, is not some mindless addiction. I am not chasing something delusional, nor am I obsessed with seven good-looking men from South Korea. I am simply chasing happiness and holding onto it, and that is a good thing.

Loving myself journey

In spring of 2021 I had dived deeper into the *Love Myself* series and went on my 'loving myself' journey that I never thought I would need to take so seriously. I became more conscious of what kind of people I was surrounding myself with, more considerate of what kind of content online is healthy for me to consume, and what isn't. I became braver to reach out to my family and friends when I had a hard time or a stress overload due to the amount of work for graduation. I rediscovered the joy of performing even if it was mostly online, I had more energy to prepare for my final piano recital and pull off all my assignments. I worked hard, but did not ignore the need for resting time either. I set myself rather realistic and achievable goals, rather than aiming for perfection in all areas and then downplaying my self-worth for not being able to do it all. I made myself celebrate all the achievements, big and small, mine and everyone else's around me. I realised that I could use the strength and support that every community I belong to provides, and found joy in rooting for my friends whenever they achieved something great.

In June, the summer holiday finally began and I almost had my master's degree in my hands. I felt like I wouldn't have been able to do this whole year without BTS and ARMY, who are always rooting for each other, always ready to help and support, to defend, to cheer each other up, and cheer for each other in every step of this weary life. Little by little, I felt my mind relaxing and letting in thoughts and ideas that I forgot I've ever had. I realised that I don't have to stay in this professional field only because I have been in it for the last 20 years, and while I still love it very much, there is so much left to discover in this life. I finally was free and capable to do whatever I want and become whoever I want to be.

"Shine, dream, smile"[3]

After the BTS' *Sowoozoo Muster* concert, I cried a good number of tears and admitted to myself that all this time I was scared to dream about the big things I want to do in my life and have been going on autopilot for quite a while. I did not regret getting a master's degree in piano performance, but I felt that I am so much more than a pianist in this narrow field of classical music. It took me two nights in a row to listen to BTS sing *Mikrokosmos* about how we as humans are big, important, and fascinating, to start feeling like I am a universe myself within the bigger universe. The lyrics "Some lights are ambition / Some lights are wanderings"[3] freed me from the pressure to come up with a plan right away after graduating, and I confidently became a "wandering universe" until I can be sure what my next ambition is.[3] "Shine, dream, smile"[3] also became my life motto, making me chase not only happiness but also my dreams, and always remembering to shine bright in the darkest nights.[3] Compared to my childhood dreams and aspirations, which were so strongly driven by my environment and the trope of serving others, these dreams were quite self-centred and selfish. I started thinking about how I can shape my life and career around what I love to do—writing, singing, dancing, playing, and composing music, finding art in everything, and creating it out of nothing. As abstract as it sounds, maybe my all over the place scattered hobbies did not have to just stay hobbies, because I truly always felt the most alive when I did them. Wouldn't more people around me actually be happier if I did what I am passionate about instead of respectfully following given roles by the society around me? Same as BTS who just did what they loved to do without thinking of a certain final goal, these days I am letting myself do what I like and doing what gives me energy, even though I did not know where it might lead me. I am gradually becoming more confident with the smallest things in life, such as choosing more out-of-comfort-zone looks for my appearance, buying what most would call useless things for adults (for example, plushies) for the first time in my life, carrying a couple of BTS' photocards in my phone case just because it's fun and may let me meet another ARMY in public, and many, many more little changes that are still making me happier every single day.

I have never had thoughts about not wanting to exist in this world, because I've always loved life and being alive, but sometimes it can become too heavy to carry it on my own. It often has felt only natural to follow my first instinct and hide, stop showing my talent, dim my light, trying to wait out the difficult times in the dark. Just like my homeland did during all those occupation years—Lithuania dimmed its light to survive the difficult times, which makes it so hard to ignite it now times are different. Yet BTS telling me "Don't disappear / because you are one great existence"[3] makes me feel a lot more important and fascinating solely because of something so natural and simple as existing. It's one thing to hear fictional characters in movies and TV shows say such things, for example, the Doctor in *Doctor Who* always telling his companions how important they are and how every life in this universe is a miracle. But it's a completely different thing to hear it from real life people like BTS members, who have already succeeded so much. BTS makes everyone, luckily me included now, believe that their existence is impressive. And I believe now too that I am impressive—impressive, unique, and important.

References

1. The Divine Mercy. (2022). *St. Maria Faustina Kowalska*. https://www.thedivinemercy.org/message/stfaustina
2. BTS (2020). 00:00 (Zero O'Clock) [song]. On M*ap of the soul: 7*. Big Hit Entertainment; doolset lyrics. (2021 Sept 12). *00:00 (Zero O'Clock)* [Translation]. https://doolsetbangtan.wordpress.com/2020/02/21/zero-oclock/
3. BTS (2019). Mikrokosmos [song]. On *Map of the soul: Persona*. Big Hit Entertainment; doolset lyrics. (2021 Sept 12). 소우주 *(Mikrokosmos)* [Translation]. https://doolsetbangtan.wordpress.com/2019/04/13/mikrokosmos/

The most magical moment in life

Michelle Bùi Hoàng

내겐 불러줄 이름이 없어.
"I don't have a name to be called by".[1]

I FIRST STUMBLED ACROSS BTS when I was on YouTube searching for a comforting Kim Jong Kook ballad. In a strange twist of fate, instead of typing in Jong Kook that day, I unknowingly typed Jung Kook in the search bar instead. Without even looking twice, I clicked on the first video that appeared, but intuitively knew that something was different when I heard the breathy vocals. The pitch was completely different to Jong Kook's and the voice, it was so smooth and bright. For some inexplicable reason, instead of closing the video like I normally would have, this voice kept me enthralled and listening on. A proper glimpse of the screen told me the song's name was *Begin* and the actual singer was Jung Kook from BTS. Who exactly was this Jung Kook and who was BTS? Curiously, I proceeded to look BTS up and landed on their newest hit *Blood, Sweat and Tears*. Not knowing what to expect, I pressed play and was taken aback as Bach's *Mass* drifted into my ears before transitioning into Jimin's angelic vocals. The change in musical composition, the cinematography and then the captivating match cut of Jimin reaching out put me in a trance. As I watched Jimin beckon towards me from the screen, fear permeated my body as I grasped just how much of a hold this music video had on me. It was too much; I felt like I was at the precipice of something otherworldly, and I most certainly was not ready for it. So, like a coward, I quickly closed my laptop and the door to the Magic Shop.

There are many factors that would have attributed to this strong reaction but reflecting on it now, the main culprit that would have warranted such a response was my perfectionism. Being born an Asian in Australia, the burden of being perfect often weighed on my shoulders. My parents were Vietnamese immigrants who had fled their war-torn country to start afresh in a country where they could not speak the language. Unsurprisingly, not being able to speak a country's native tongue presented many barriers for my parents. However, for their dream of giving their children better lives, they persevered. Growing up with this knowledge, I was always fuelled with the desire to be the best at everything I did to make their sacrifice worthwhile. Whether that was through being the perfect student or the perfect daughter, anything less than perfect was not good enough.

I quickly began to learn that perfection was not always so easily achieved, and sometimes maintaining it was completely out of my control. Before I started school, it had never occurred to me that my name was any different. Unsure of how naming conventions worked in a Western setting, my parents gave me a five-part name, a three-part first name and a two-part last name. My birth paperwork was nothing but a jargon of letters to them, and they were distinctly confused on what the difference between a first or middle name was. Thus, my first name, Phương Thảo Michelle was created.

As you can imagine, having a long name like that did not bode so well for a young Vietnamese girl trying to desperately fit in. My skin colour, eyes, and even lunches already made me stick out in school like a sore thumb. When I entered a world where Vietnamese was no longer the main language spoken, it quickly dawned on me that my name made me stand out for all the wrong reasons. I soon began to resent my name, as I grew wearisome of repeatedly correcting people's pronunciation and then having to fake laugh as my Caucasian classmates would make a xenophobic comment about my name. My name detracted from the perfect student image that I had created for myself, and it fed into my growing insecurity of being Asian. As a result, whenever I could, I stopped using Phương Thảo in my name. Before anyone would have a chance to even pronounce my name, I would jump in and tell them that just Michelle was fine. To become what I thought Western society deemed perfect, I carelessly threw away a part of myself.

When I was 10, my dad was diagnosed with cancer and unexpectedly, I was given a new role to play. My life suddenly became a flurry of translating for my parents at medical appointments and becoming a third parental figure to my sisters. It was a difficult time for my family and despite my dad being declared cancer free after his chemotherapy regimen not long after, he relapsed. When my dad's health deteriorated the second time, I started to lose hope. A voice would creep into my head every time I saw him in pain and whisper that it was my fault. Was I doing enough? Did I translate that one medical reference perfectly? At the time, I never stopped to question why this voice plagued my thoughts, instead, the only thing I took notice of was what it was telling me. I was failing my dad. After five long years, my dad ultimately lost his battle to cancer. To this day, I vividly remember that when it sunk in that he was truly gone and I saw all the chaos ensuing in his hospital room, the tears running down my face stopped. Immediately, I cast my feelings away into the deepest depths of my mind and went into a perfectly controlled state. Even though I had just lost my dad, the moment I saw my mother and my sisters cry, I instinctively felt that I could not. As the eldest in the family, it was ingrained in me that I had to be the strongest. My family did not need someone weak; they needed a perfect daughter and older sister. At only 15, I had felt that letting myself grieve was a weakness, so I filled the cracks of trauma with responsibility. I had failed to protect my dad so now, my responsibility was to protect my remaining family the only way I knew how, being perfect.

피울 수 없는 꽃을 키웠어.

"I raised a flower that couldn't bloom".[2]

As the internet was introduced into the modern world, I eventually uncovered the wonder that was K-pop. From DBSK, Big Bang to 2PM, I devoured K-pop as though I had been starved of music for years. I was filled with awe as I finally understood my dad's obsession with music that was in a different language. For the first time since losing him, I felt something. It connected me not just to him, but also to the world again. I watched music video after music video of people who looked just like me and couldn't wait to share this discovery with all my friends. Regrettably, the time for K-pop was not meant to be during my teenage years. Similarly, to my name, it was met with derision and disdain. My appreciation for the genre was reduced to an obsession with men who weren't 'real men', and my intellect was questioned as people around me judged me for listening to music that was not in English.

Understandably, at the peak of my teenagehood, I was more fixated on being 'cool' and accepted by my peers than standing out for enjoying Asian music, so I became embarrassed of listening to K-pop. I stopped listening to it around others in the fear that they'd think I was 'too Asian' and eventually I distanced myself from the genre completely. It became a guilty pleasure for me but one I was terrified of indulging in too often because every time I listened to it, I felt as though I was one step closer to turning into that 'obsessive' K-pop fangirl everybody warned me about. Yet whenever I was feeling vulnerable, K-pop would be the first thing I turned to. Even though I shied away from it because it was Asian, I felt so seen and comforted when I listened to it. Which is why when I heard *Blood, Sweat and Tears* for the first time, I panicked. *Blood, Sweat and Tears* evoked feelings and desires inside me that my perfectionism had kept locked up. I was brimming with curiosity but my pride stopped me and before I could fall under BTS' spell, I fled.

The years flew by, and I became more adept at shifting into what people expected of me. I was working towards a career in medicine like my parents always wanted, and I was experiencing love with another person for the first time. In Asian cultures, love is something that we often do not see expressed so most of what I knew about love at that point was the love shown in the Korean dramas that my mum and I would devour together.

Korean dramas, during my formative years, often depicted the female lead as a damsel in distress or a girl that had to overcome defying odds at her own detriment just to be with the male lead. Love was portrayed as all-consuming and when it came my way, I made it my everything. I wanted to become someone's perfect love, so naturally, like every other aspect of my life, I shaped myself into becoming what I thought his perfect love was. In my naivety, I constructed my entire world around loving one single person and when that person morphed into someone I could no longer recognise, I refused to acknowledge it. No matter how many warning signs flashed before me, how many bruises peppered my body, I pointedly ignored them, looking the other way in the name of love until my mind had enough and flushed me with my first flood of cortisol.

My first anxiety attack was a wake-up call that something was very wrong. At this point, I was so used to ignoring my own feelings that when I was forced to deal with the feelings that came with an anxiety attack, I was wildly unprepared. It awoke a beast that I had kept locked up in the darkest recesses of my mind and when it woke, it was livid. It roared and thrashed in the cage that was my mind, and I was utterly helpless at stopping its onslaught. At the time, I didn't understand why the beast was so angry at me. I had done everything that everyone expected of me to perfection. Wasn't it enough? My anxiety gradually paved the way for the beast to become a more prominent figure in my mind. Instead of going back into its dark corner like it usually did, it stayed, hissing my worst fears every hour of every day.

Denial became my defence mechanism to the beast; I didn't want to face my fears, nor did I want to admit to having any. Depression was something that just did not fit in with the perfect persona that I had painstakingly constructed for the world, so I denied its existence. The battle inside of my head raged on as the years passed and scars both inside and outside began to decorate my weary body. No matter what mask I put on, what role I played, nothing could satiate the beast's fury. Just like the lyrics in *FAKE LOVE* said, I had been erasing myself and making myself into everyone else's doll. [2] I was unsure of who I had become over the years, and each time I stared at myself in the mirror; I became more and more perplexed at who exactly was looking back at me.

Perfectionism in literature has been found as a vulnerability factor for inducing depression and anxiety along with many other psychological issues in individuals because of the "magnitude of dissatisfaction they live with every day".[3] It can manifest into two different forms, adaptive and maladaptive, the latter being characterised by the individual consistently comparing themselves with an 'ideal' person, being controlled by others opinions and obsessively thinking about their own failures.[4] These individuals often "underestimate their own performance"[4] leading to feelings such as guilt, shame, fear of judgment and low self-esteem.[4] In particular, studies have indicated that Asians often display perfectionistic traits because of acculturation and interdependence between interpersonal relationships, obligations, responsibilities, and resultantly, a propensity to tie one's meaning of self to those relationships.[5]

During my early 20s, whenever I displayed any type of 'negative' emotion, it was trivialised, or I was punished for feeling such things in the first place. Repeatedly, it was drilled into me that to be loved, I had to don a mask and become the perfect version of myself that everyone else saw. From feelings of sadness to feelings of fear, I became so ashamed of having these feelings that I would try to push them down and box them up as soon as any hint of them crept up. Deep down, I think I knew that I was depressed but I kept trying to convince myself otherwise. In the early stages of my depression, I was volatile and frequently used any and every kind of poison to paralyse the beast roaring in my head. Unsurprisingly, this was not a sustainable solution and made it blatantly obvious to everyone around me that something was wrong. I distinctly remember the looks of concern and judgment that I received at the time, and I loathed it. I hated that my depression had driven me to become a person with such visible flaws, so in my desperation I began to compartmentalise all over again. I crawled and performed my way through the greatest show I have ever put on, all so that everyone could see me the way I wanted to be seen again. The only trouble was that once I started, I could not stop. As Suga said in *Outro: Her*, "I can never take off the mask, because the me behind this mask, is not the one you know".[6] Consequently, keeping up the façade around everyone wore on me. I desperately wanted to stop the performance, but my perfectionism would not let me.

넌 절벽 끝에 서 있던 내 마지막 이유야. Live.

"You're the last reason for me who was standing on the edge of a cliff. Live".[7]

Eventually, the day came when I lost the will to fight against the beast anymore. I was so achingly tired of chasing after perfection, and I yearned for the roaring in my head to permanently cease.

So, that very night, I conceded. I sat in my kitchen clutching my pocket utility knife, a knife that had become a familiar companion to me over the years. For once, the beast that ravaged my mind was quiet. It was as though the beast knew that our joint suffering was about to end and that it too was waiting patiently to be set free. As I slid the blade out, I started reflecting on different moments of my life and then the most peculiar moment crossed my mind. I remembered the day I saw Jimin reaching out to me in *Blood, Sweat and Tears*. I wondered at the time why on earth this memory resurfaced, but it was enough to make me pause momentarily and go look up BTS on my phone. Being a millennial who grew up in the golden age of Harry Potter, naturally I gravitated towards the song titled *Magic Shop*. It was nothing more than a simple lyric music video but just like in *Blood, Sweat and Tears*, I was beguiled. My heart ached as, verse by verse, the BTS members spoke to a long-forgotten part of my soul. Perhaps it was fate or serendipity as some may say, but for the second time, Jimin reached out and invited me into the Magic Shop.

"Let's make a door in your heart
Open the door and this place will await
It's okay to believe, the Magic Shop will comfort you". [7]

The use of the Magic Shop goes as far back as the 1950s and has been used as a method where a therapist can masquerade as a shopkeeper and encourage their "customer" to barter psychological wares that they may want to get rid of for something entirely different.[8,9] BTS' Magic Shop draws on this concept and takes further inspiration from James R. Doty's book, *Into the Magic Shop*, a memoir in which he explores the power of positive thinking and mindfulness. In his novel, James reminisces on his childhood as a boy living without hope and how his entire life altered its course, the day he stepped into a magic shop.[10] Similarly, that night when I stepped into BTS' Magic Shop, my life also began to alter its course.

In the *Fake Love* trailer, the Magic Shop was described as "a psychodramatic technique that exchanges fear for a positive attitude"[11] and Jung Kook later explained in an interview that *Magic Shop* was a song for "when ARMY are tired, emotionally exhausted and having a rough time".[12] It was a song written for ARMY to let them know that BTS would always be there for them and that BTS would "be the strength for when they feel down".[12] Somehow, when I needed them the most, 8381 kms away, BTS heard my soul's pleas and exchanged my fear of living for their comfort.

Like most ARMY, when I fell into the rabbit hole that was the BTS universe, I was struck with an insatiable desire to consume every morsel of content they had to offer. Up until this point, I had mostly consumed their music but then, I came across their *Burn the Stage* documentary film. For me, the most unforgettable moment of that film was watching Jimin cry in frustration backstage as he adamantly told the staff that he had messed up his solo performance on stage. Curious to see just how messed up this performance was, I went to watch said solo and was bewildered as I could not pick up where his voice had supposedly cracked. Switching back to the film, Jimin then explained that he always felt extreme amounts of stress prior to his solo performances due to the overwhelming pressure to do well and how even one mistake could become unbearable for him.[13] I was floored listening to his confession as suddenly, I saw myself reflected in him. My entire life, I had lived with the fervent belief that being perfect was the only way to command respect and receive love. Any mistake, no matter how big or small, always haunted me and acted as sustenance for the beast. Every interaction, action, and thought I had was heavily governed by my perfectionism, which meant that anything I did was constantly short of perfect.

The day that I watched Jimin in *Burn the Stage,* my heart broke not just for him, but for me as well. I wept and wept as I remembered the little girl who stopped using her real name, the teenager who stopped listening to K-pop and the young woman who almost erased herself completely because of the insidious beast that was brought to life from perfectionism. The connection that I shared with Jimin in that fleeting moment altered something inside of me. It touched a part of my soul that I had never shared with the world before. I felt safe because I could wholly be myself without any fear of rejection. For the first time in a long time, a kernel of light appeared as I saw myself in Jimin's shoes. I realised that if I felt nothing but sadness and love for him in the moment that his world was crashing down from his own perfectionist tendencies, perhaps others thought the same when it came to me. Not so long after watching this, Jimin gifted ARMY with a self-composed track, one that was inspired by his struggles of being true to himself. He explained in one of his VLives that he often thought that he wasn't good enough and struggled by himself, but through this song he wanted to comfort people who were in a similar situation.[14] His raw earnestness finally brought my roaring brain to a stop as he echoed what I had felt inside so without hesitation, I stuck out my pinkie and made him a promise.

Making the decision to start loving myself was the hardest thing I ever decided to do. In *Break the Silence*, Jimin said, "I think I realised a lot of things when it comes to loving yourself. I think it's about asking yourself a lot of questions and learning more about who you are. I think that's the foundation and beginning of learning to love yourself."[15] There were many perfectionist walls that I had erected over the years to fit into a xenophobic world, and making my way back to who I was and accepting myself intimidated me. Who was the real me? How was I supposed to love myself? I didn't know. To me, being a perfectionist wasn't just about not making a mistake, it was also the tying of my self-worth to my achievements and people's opinions of me. When it came to loving myself, the biggest test was acknowledging and letting go of that tie.

As an Asian Australian with immigrant Vietnamese parents, my upbringing was very much influenced by Confucianism. High value was placed on filial piety, and academic excellence was equated to bringing 'honour' to one's family.[16] I grew up thinking that if I wanted to be successful, I had to work in healthcare. That expectation, coupled with my dad passing away from cancer, gave me the conviction that for me to succeed and in turn be happy in life, I needed to not become a doctor but a radiation therapist. Admittedly in the beginning, I was starry eyed, I was confident that I had made a conscious choice of my own in not becoming a doctor. A career that I chose felt like a solid first step to loving myself and at the same time, a way to atone for not being able to save my dad all those years ago. The only problem was this particular career path exacerbated my perfectionism.

Radiation therapy is a field that not many people would know of unless their lives have been touched by cancer. In my role as a radiation therapist, there were two distinct sides. The treatment side was where I was responsible for delivering radiation treatment to cancer patients. While the planning side was where I was responsible for designing treatment plans that were a fine balance between eradicating a patient's cancer and preventing unnecessary radiation dose to their healthy tissue. Radiation once delivered to the human body is unable to be reversed and so, that left little to no room for mistakes as unnecessary radiation could then lead to secondary cancers down the track.[17] Unsurprisingly, my brain was constantly whirring with ways in which I could ensure this would not happen and no matter how well received my work was, the perfectionist in me was never satisfied. Working in a field where patients were going through cancer also meant that a major component of my work demanded that I provide them with emotionally focussed care. Day in and day out, I was faced with patients in emotional pain, distress, or suffering and every day I gave away a small piece of myself. It seems ironic now that I delivered a presentation to my colleagues about emotional burnout but did not recognise that I was suffering from the symptoms myself.

It was found in Blanchard et al.'s study, that within medical disciplines, burnout was prominent in oncology disciplines due to factors such as unrealistic expectations of patients, a greater number of losses due to the types of patients encountered and the sense of failure that ensued because of these losses.[18] To the outside eye, I was doing remarkably well but every night I couldn't help but wonder why I felt like a failure. I had succeeded in becoming a radiation therapist, I was making a difference to people's lives ,and yet it felt like I was drowning. The fulfillment I had expected to come, didn't. All these years and I was still caught in a lie.

On one of those 'just get through today' kind of days, one of my colleagues voiced her frustration with my name and asked me why my parents had made it so complicated. At the time I laughed off her comment but as the day went by, that interaction gnawed at me. It's strange that even when many years may have passed, moments from your childhood can resurface at the drop of a hat. Suddenly, I was back in my primary school classroom, looking down towards the ground as other students in my class laughed and told me to get a real name. My co-worker's offhand comment triggered a cascade of memories in me. Memories of other colleagues repeatedly getting my name wrong, of comments about me looking the same as other Asian colleagues in the department, and of being told that I couldn't take a joke when I tried to speak up. These memories brought back the beast's voice in my head with a vengeance and reminded me again that I was never going to be enough.

어제의 나 오늘의 나 내일의 나. 빠짐없이 남김없이 모두 다 나.

"Yesterday's me, today's me, tomorrow's me. Without exception,

all together they are me".[19]

It was around this time that a VLive notification for Jimin popped up, and impulsively I typed in the chat how suffocated and alone I felt. It was entirely out of character for me to do something like that but knowing that no one would know who I was, I felt an innate sense of relief at just being able to express myself. During this V Live, Jimin sang *Promise, Love Myself,* and *Magic Shop.*

"Promise me now
Even if you feel alone many times a day, don't throw yourself away.
Pause for a moment right here, hook your pinkie with mine and promise me now[20]
Let's be honest and admit what we have to admit that your standards are more strict when they are applied to you[19]
You gave me the best of me
So, you'll give you the best of you"[7]

Tears that I had been inadvertently holding fell as he sung those songs, and then he held his pinky up to the screen. I stared back and this time, a different memory resurfaced. The memory of the promise I made him. Had I really been giving myself the best of myself? Was I loving myself? The stark realisation hit that my perfectionism was still very much in control and even though I thought my career was what I wanted, it clicked in that moment that I didn't choose it because I wanted it. I chose it because radiation therapy was still a medical discipline, which meant I wouldn't be disappointing my mum completely. I chose it because of the trauma I had buried over the years about failing my dad, and I kept choosing it because I wanted to save all those people from experiencing the pain and loss I felt over the years. The love of others, my happiness, I viewed it all as a transaction that could only be earned through taking care of others' needs because I never believed that I was worthy. Hands trembling at this epiphany, I began typing in my search bar as Jimin ended his live with, "I want to say good job to all of you. Because you are trying very hard now. Starting from tomorrow and from this moment, only happy moments will come to ARMY" and I did something I never willingly did before, I chose myself. [21]

Walking alongside BTS, I never felt alone as every step of the way their voices became my wings. The wings that guided me to therapy, to facing myself, and to embracing the not so perfect parts of me. In 2018, RM proudly introduced himself as Kim Namjoon at the United Nations and said unabashedly to the world, "I have many faults and I have many fears, but I am going to embrace myself as hard as I can, and I'm starting to love myself, little by little". [22] I remember at the time, his stark vulnerability and cultural pride brought tears to my eyes, as he made me truly believe that his voice mattered, and that maybe, my voice could matter too. For so long, my identity had been taken away from me for other people's happiness and I had spent so much time tying my self-worth to those relationships that I had neglected the most important one of all, the one with myself.

Through their Love Yourself trilogy, BTS gave me the keys to start truly understanding myself and to finding a new way forward. [23] RM taught me that everything goes, Jin taught me self-confidence, Suga taught me to not be afraid of the darkness, j-hope taught me to how to hope, Jimin taught me how to love, V taught me self-acceptance and Jung Kook taught me how to dream. Together, the seven of them lit up the dark night so that I could find a way to shine, dream and smile. From my wonderfully unique three-part name that no one else in the world owned to the BTS fangirling that gave me a bulletproof community; all those things that I had resented so much about myself in the past, BTS made them become the very reasons I learned to love myself.

To this day, my perfectionism still rears its ugly head, but it no longer swallows me whole as it once did. On the days that it makes me want to disappear, I open the door to the Magic Shop and remember all the blood, sweat, and tears that I had spilled to find that galaxy inside of me. The memories that haunted me in the past were gradually replaced with new ones that BTS helped me make. The memories of staying silent became one where I spoke myself and stood up against racism. The memory of living someone else's dream became one where I found the courage to quit my job and write this story. The memory of hiding my interests and hobbies became the memory of letting go of other's perceptions and embracing being ARMY and being myself. In 2022, I rewatched RM's speech at the United Nations again but this time, I did not shed any tears. This time when RM asked, "what is your name?"[22] I answered back with Phương Thảo Michelle.

And I could have sworn, that in that magical moment, there was "a person in Korea, in the city of Seoul",[24] that smiled and whispered back, "you showed me".[7]

References

1 BTS (2018). 전하지 못한 진심 (The Truth Untold) Ft. Steve Aoki [Song]. On *BTS - Love Yourself 轉 'Tear'*. Big Hit Entertainment.; Doolset. (2018). 전하지 못한 진심 (The Truth Untold) Ft. Steve Aoki *(English Translation)*. https://doolsetbangtan.wordpress.com/2018/06/01/the-truth-untold-ft-steve-aoki/

2 BTS (2018). FAKE LOVE [Song]. On *BTS - Love Yourself 轉 'Tear'*. Big Hit Entertainment.; Genius. (2022). *BTS - FAKE LOVE (English Translation)*. https://genius.com/Genius-english-translations-bts-fake-love-english-translation-lyrics

3 Melrose, S. (2011). Perfectionism and depression: vulnerabilities nurses need to understand. *Nursing Research and Practice*.

4 Oros, L. B., Iourno, O., & Serppe, M. (2017). Child perfectionism and its relationship with personality, excessive parental demands, depressive symptoms and experience of positive emotions. *The Spanish Journal of Psychology, 20*.

5 Yoon, J., & Lau, A. S. (2008). Maladaptive perfectionism and depressive symptoms among Asian American college students: contributors of interdependence and parental relations. *Cultural Diversity & Ethnic Minority Psychology, 14*(2), 92-101.

6 BTS (2017). Outro: Her [Song]. On *BTS- Love Yourself 承 'Her'*. Big Hit Entertainment.; Genius. (2022). *BTS - "Outro: Her" (English Translation)*. https://genius.com/Genius-english-translations-bts-outro-her-english-translation-lyrics

7 BTS (2018). Magic Shop [Song]. On *BTS - Love Yourself 轉 'Tear'*. Big Hit Entertainment.; Genius. (2022). *BTS - Magic Shop (English Translation)*. https://genius.com/Genius-english-translations-bts-magic-shop-english-translation-lyrics

[8] Koile, E. (2011). The Magic Shop: the therapist masquerades as a shopkeeper. *Voices: The Art and Science of Psychotherapy*, 6-18.

[9] Barbour, A. (1992). Purpose and strategy behind the magic shop. *Journal of Group Psychotherapy, Psychodrama & Sociometry, 45*(3), 91-101.

[10] Doty, J. R. (2017). *Into the Magic Shop: A Neurosurgeon's Quest to Discover the Mysteries of the Brain and the Secrets of the Heart.* New York City: Avery Publishing Group.

[11] HYBE LABELS. (2015, May 15). BTS (방탄소년단) 'FAKE LOVE' Official Teaser 1 [Video]. YouTube. https://www.youtube.com/watch?v=BP71K87Hp5Y&list=RDBP71K87Hp5Y&start_radio=1

[12] Pitchfork. (2020, October 6). BTS Break Down Their Albums, From DARK & WILD to MAP OF THE SOUL : 7 | Pitchfork [Video]. YouTube. https://www.youtube.com/watch?v=Tt9x61AL50E&t=683s

[13] BANGTANTV. (2018). Burn the Stage: The Movie [Video]. YouTube. Retrieved from https://www.youtube.com/watch?v=YgG9f4MJ1eU

[14] BTS. (2019). BTS Live : 내가 왔다! [Video]. V Live. https://www.vlive.tv/video/109729

[15] Big Hit Entertainment. (n.d.). Break the Silence: The Movie [Video]. *2020*. Weverse. https://www.weverse.io/bts/media/4827

[16] Bedford, O., & Yeh, K. (2019). The History and the Future of the Psychology of Filial Piety: Chinese Norms to Contextualized Personality Construct. *Frontiers in Psychology, 10*(100).

[17] Dracham, C. B., Shankar, A., & Madan, R. (2018). Radiation induced secondary malignancies: a review article. *Radiation Oncology Journal, 36*(2), 85–94.

[18] Blanchard, P., Truchot, D., Albiges-Sauvin, L., Dewas, S., Pointreau, Y., Rodrigues, M., et al. (2010). Prevalence and causes of burnout

amongst oncology residents: A comprehensive nationwide cross-sectional study. *European Journal of Cancer. 46*(15), 2708-15.

[19] BTS (2018). Answer: Love Myself [Song]. On ***BTS - LOVE YOURSELF 結 'Answer'***. Big Hit Entertainment.; Doolset. (2018). Answer: Love Myself *(English Translation)*. https://doolsetbangtan.wordpress.com/2018/08/24/answer-love-myself/

[20] BTS (2018). 약속 (Promise) [Song]. On *SoundCloud Releases*. Big Hit Entertainment.; Doolset. (2018). 약속 (Promise, Jimin) *(English Translation)*. https://doolsetbangtan.wordpress.com/2018/12/30/promise-jimin/

[21] BTS. (2021). BTS Live : 내가 왔다! [Video]. V Live. https://www.vlive.tv/post/0-25056764

[22] UNICEF. (2018, September 25). BTS speech at the United Nations | UNICEF [Video]. YouTube. https://www.youtube.com/watch?v=oTe4f-bBEKg

[23] Eaglehawk, W. (2020). *Idol Limerence: the art of loving BTS as phenomena*. Revolutionaries.

[24] BANGTANTV. (2020, June 08). BTS Commencement Speech | Dear Class Of 2020 [Video]. YouTube. https://www.youtube.com/watch?v=AU6uF5sFtwA&t=447s

My name is Ran: A not so lonely gender journey

Ran Rice (he/him)

THE STATE OF knowing one's self is still new to me. By this I mean, I barely knew what my own name was until just about a year ago. It took me over two decades to begin to feel as though I knew how I wanted the world to address me, to perceive me. It took me over two decades to become aware of how I wanted to perceive myself. Yet, despite these newfound convictions, I wonder how one can have such an unerring sense of who they are. I avoid this question constantly, yet I think about it frequently; a simultaneous push that has me running and a pull to keep me in orbit. This running in circles is not my favourite activity, but it seems to keep me busy; a practice that has become a socially acceptable excuse to forget who you are, to stop caring about yourself as an individual. To stop 'loving yourself'.

Am I really ARMY?

> "*I am afraid, I am miserable, I'm so afraid that you, too might leave me again in the end"*
>
> –*The Truth Untold,* BTS[1]

Am I really ARMY? I ask this because I am unable to say that I witnessed BTS' debut in June of 2013. I cannot say that I knew the answer to the crossword puzzle prompt three down, their 2013 debut single (three words),[2] without having to look it up. I most definitely do not know all of their birthdays by heart. I'm not very good at learning the dances to the songs or memorising the fan chants for the concerts. I felt as though the back and forth between making a decision on who my bias was meant I didn't actually have a true bias. It took me more than two months to grasp 한글 and even then I'm still barely moving through the rest of the 한국어 lessons. I haven't watched all of their VLives and was unsure of how to know when they were even happening. I do not have very many social media accounts, and the ones I do have, I am not incredibly active on. I do not have an ARMY membership and I haven't seriously considered ever getting one. I find it really hard to justify spending money on merchandise or fan created products, even when I really want them or want to support other fans. Sometimes, I hit shuffle on a playlist that doesn't include their music. Despite these doubts, I have quickly come to learn that it doesn't take all of these things to be ARMY. Not everyone can speak Korean, or wants to be active on social media sites. There are others who don't want to financially invest in the experience, or are simply unable to. Maybe it's possible to be ARMY in aspects other than these. A comforting thought, I would soon discover to be very true.

Nevertheless, the reasons were beginning to feel endless and unforgiving. Yet the most important counterargument to my existence as a part of this fanbase is that I do not have any ARMY friends. The most prominent reason as to why I ask myself daily if I am really ARMY is because I do not *know* ARMY.

ARMY is said to be many things, but most prominently it is said to be big. In the millions. And yet, I feel alone. I am not sure how many reasons I have created to make sense of it all. *You aren't prominent on social media, so they probably can't find you. You don't live in a big city where most of the fans live, so they probably can't find you. You don't stand out enough, so they probably can't find you.* These are just excuses, excuses that progressively hurt the more my brain can come up with them. In my personal opinion, the most notable and likely to be correct is that maybe I am not the ideal fan. Therefore, it's not that they can't find me, rather they simply don't care to find me. This is really all I can think about of late, ARMY does not know who I am, ARMY doesn't even know my name.

ARMY is said to be many things, but I am having a really hard time believing the voice inside my head that tells me this is how it is supposed to be. I am afraid of *The Truth Untold*. But the common denominator here is me. I am not an ideal fan, even in the discussion around ARMY you hear terms like 'fangirl' that personally don't resonate with me. As a queer, transmasculine, and gender non-conforming fan, I'm afraid I find most gendered descriptions of ARMY unrelatable. I especially feel left out of most fan edits or references to the fanbase that rely solely on the use of 'she' and 'her' gendered pronouns.

Even as I write this I have a hard time putting my identity descriptors on paper, to me they are fluid and always changing. I know most people prefer to have definitive answers when it comes to things like who I am and how I see myself. For me, that's a nearly impossible task, I may never have these answers. Not only have I made peace with that, I've also made peace with the fact that it's something others may never be able to make peace with. When I asked a friend what the non-binary term for fangirl was I received an even more devastating response, something along the lines of 'I think, just fan'. For me, it would have been less disconcerting if the word 'just' hadn't been included, but how am I supposed to explain that to those who quite possibly will never be able to understand those feelings? How do I express how desperately I wish to not be labeled as 'just a fan'? Although these thoughts mostly came to the forefront of my mind when I first found BTS, the concern has always been steadily increasing. Especially now, as I move more confidently through my gender journey, having completed some gender-affirming surgery and exploring gender-affirming hormone therapy options. So needless to say, other questions of concern arise for me as I move along.

Am I concerned about facing homophobia and transphobia within this fanbase? Of course. But I'm concerned with facing those systems of oppression every day amongst all people. I have my own reasons to believe that the good in ARMY will outweigh anything else I am confronted with. Even with this sense of hope, I don't believe finding it hard to relate to the overall concept of being ARMY means that I cannot identify as ARMY at all. I may at times feel unwelcome or as though I do not belong but a lot of those feelings are a result of the self-doubt I experience, and quite possibly the misrepresentation of ARMY as a whole.

It would be inaccurate for me to assume that other ARMY around the world haven't had similar experiences as myself, even if not identical. Although there are similarities to be found amongst ARMY, we know ARMY is diverse and made up of all walks of life, with unique and individual experiences, each with a story to tell. Despite being armed with this promising sentiment, I know I am not an ideal fan. I do not wish to cause a big enough ripple and upset the precarious balance that exists between idol and fan. The possibility that it might not be my place is daunting, and knowing this is a heavy burden to carry.

The idol and the fan

> *"What is your name, whether you have anywhere to go, oh could you tell me?"*
>
> –*The Truth Untold*, BTS[1]

By definition, dichotomies and binaries are black and white. The differences in the shades in between can be too much to understand, and therefore it has been easier to simply leave them out of the picture. This lack of understanding and clarity has forced many people into boxes that fail to accurately define who they are and take into account individual experiences. This is something that cultural theory strives to do by "bring[ing] together the critical analysis of cultural meanings with the careful consideration of material practices. While focusing on specific events, they keep the historical horizon in clear view; even while considering intimate relations and experiences, they attend to those changes in production, consumption, technology, and law that set the stage for everyday life".[4] The many possibilities that moving away from binaries as fact can bring to people and our social environment are a multitude and can be promising and beneficial for many lives. This process would give us the opportunity to analyse and validate those different shades of grey, as well as give light to the plethora of colours that make up who we all are. An example of this and a mighty comforting takeaway for me, was in *Idol Limerence: The Art of Loving BTS as Phenomena* when Wallea Eaglehawk describes ARMY as being post-gender and sharing love as one common language.[3]

One lens that could be applied is transgender studies. Talking intersectionally is something that transgender studies does well, an extension off of feminist studies and feminist theory and related in many ways to queer theory. Not only does transgender studies open the conversation into thinking outside the dichotomy, it also invites us to actively take what we know and feel and apply it to the real world, the political spectre, and social policy. Transgender studies "investigate questions of embodied difference, and analyse how such differences are transformed into social hierarchies—without ever losing sight of the fact that "difference" and "hierarchy" are never mere abstractions; they are systems of power that operate on actual bodies, capable of producing pain and pleasure, health and sickness, punishment and reward, life and death".[5] The idol and fan dichotomy is one of the more difficult binaries I've recently studied, next to gender. Interestingly enough, I find myself once again contemplating the reality of such a juxtaposition:

> An idol has more power than a fan who got them to where they are. No matter how much an idol may love their fans, the inequalities remain. An idol can only be an idol within a capitalistic society; an idol can only exist at the expense of their fans. One is powerful and the other, less so. One makes a profit from the other, and rarely is it the other

> way around. It only remains ethical for as long as the fan willingly participates, but that in itself is up for debate.[3]

It is in dissecting these binaries that I am once again confronted with my own personal binary battle. "I want my body to exist in the same genderless hell as my mind." Words spoken in a rush and flood of emotions. It's a fleeting memory of mine, however the impact it had was almost unbearable. Words spoken to someone with authority, someone with the power to decide whether or not I have the right to exist as a person on this planet and just in general. It may seem too literal to some, but to me it is a very serious matter. If they had chosen differently, I am not so sure I would be here to tell you so. I also never knew that in speaking the words so much in my life would change so quickly. So for the longest time, I never did speak them aloud. I only ever wrote them. When those words and many others like them finally fell from my lips, I was no longer able to stop them. I could see who I was in the distance, but I was having such a difficult time deciding if it was too light or too dark for me to see. I wasn't focusing on the fact that it wasn't going to be a discernible image either way. But I knew I was close, and so I decided I wasn't going to let others dictate my existence even though I know they play a major role in doing so.

And yet, I am here. The only person I can thank for that is myself. A sentence I never thought I would utter until very recently. More on that in a moment. For now, I can only think about how I am here and yet not many people know that. One could argue that the important people know, the people who matter know. What about those who matter to me? Do they know I am here? Do they know my name? I know their names;

BTS and ARMY. But I've never been more certain that they do not know my name than I am now.

So when Jack Halberstam asks, "what is in a name?"[6] I listen. Although the question allows for the follow-up of a wide range and variety of fascinating theories, I wish to first focus on 'how' is a name. This comes from the discussion in Halberstam's piece *Trans** which offers the explanation that naming, and the crucial value that is applied to it, resulted from the implications of colonialism; colonial expansion and colonial enterprise.[6] The original aspect, although applied to plants, very quickly made a transition to humans and thus to gender and sexuality and many things beyond.[6] This introduction of the naming process in relation to gender and sexuality and other aspects of human life changes the way in which people understand and interpret the world around them and its inhabitants. In many ways, this introduction was a positive and progressive change to the way in which we define who we are as people. Yet with all good things comes the less good things, after the naming process was introduced, the idea of applying specific labels to different forms of identity became prevalent.

In the Netflix show titled *Dear White People* (2017)[7] the exploration of labels is a big part of the story line. At one point in the show the character, "Lionel responds to Silvio's assumption [of his sexuality] by saying, 'I really don't subscribe to those kinds of labels.' 'Those labels keep people in Florida from drinking Windex,' Silvio says".[8] This interaction leads to a very similar although much more light-hearted discussion about the different views people in the LGBTQ+ community have over what labels can do for us. While some people find comfort with themselves in labels, some are limited by them and may even feel trapped, and others will drink Windex without them. Labelling has a way of grouping people together, an aspect that should be a positive thing, until we realise that some groups have labels that change the criteria of what it means to be able to belong. Although Halberstam does a great job of creating the critique of labels from a mostly LGBTQ+ perspective while still keeping intersectionality in mind, I hesitate to limit this view point.

What is realised throughout the writing of Halberstam is that there are positives and negatives to naming, labelling, and identities. The reality of the situation is that the discussion of naming and labels may not have been as crucial as it is to this kind of theory if it hadn't been for the names and labels in the first place. So "the answer to the question "what's in a name?" is "Everything!""[6] The 'how' and the 'what' of the name question offer a lot to think about, yet I still have no answer to the 'why.' Why do we go through the effort of naming and labelling? If 'everything' is in a name, why is that?

I like to think that if everything is in a name, then that would also imply that nothing is in name. The 'everything' that exists in names exists only because we as humans have placed it in that name through discourse and the implications of value. For a name to mean nothing, we simply remove its value, we remove it from the conversation, or we add it to the conversation with different meaning; much like the reclaiming of words. The names and labels do not cause nearly as much damage as do the meanings that are attached to them and the amount of value that we place in them. An entertaining game called social construction.

In other words, it begins to make sense why it would feel so life changing and incredibly important for others to not only know I am here, but to know my name. Not just the important people, the people who matter. More specifically, the people who matter *to me*. I would like to think it could balance out the binary of idol and fan if maybe they knew my name. I do not think it has the ability to erase the power that exists between the two, to change the immensely beneficial hierarchy capitalism insists on keeping in place. Nevertheless, I do believe it could bring about a calm between the relationship that maybe wasn't present before. As Eaglehawk states, "so when idol and fan come together they become the literal embodiment of love, an encounter with God, or the divine itself".[3] In my mind, if they knew my name, the scale that is so heavily weighed one way or the other wouldn't balance out completely. But it would shift, ever so slightly. The carefully laid foundation of the idol and fan dichotomy would receive its first crack. A thin line that starts at the very top edge of the foundation. Barely perceivable to a passerby, and yet it exists.

A Critique of loneliness

> "*Full of loneliness, this garden bloomed... Bloomed in a garden of loneliness, a flower that resembles you*"
>
> –*The Truth Untold*, BTS[1]

Take for example this essay. The reason this essay exists is because it was requested in response to RM stating that he wanted to know our stories as fans, who we are and how we came to be knocking on their door asking for answers no one has to questions society doesn't want us to ask. I could tell him that story. I could tell all seven of them my story. However, when I am done writing it, when the soft clicks of the keyboard end and I confidently place the last punctuation mark, I will still be alone and he will still not know my name. None of them will.

The more I think about it and the more the fear claws its way up my esophagus stopping the words from being spoken, I think to myself that I would rather tell Echo my story.[3] I think about Echo's story and how I found so many different aspects of it relatable in my own way but more so, all I could think about was wanting to meet Echo. Wanting to tell Echo my name and reciprocate Echo's story with my own story. I want to be friends with Echo. I think we could be really good friends. It only took but one sentence for all of the pieces to come together once again: "...the fictitious life of Echo who is the physical embodiment of ARMY".[3] There it was; *The Truth Untold*. I didn't really want to talk to Echo, I wanted to talk to ARMY. I still want to talk to ARMY.

I no longer wish to feel as though I am standing in the midst of a sea of people in purple who have lives, who have dreams, who matter, and feel as though I am not allowed to be a part of it all. Thinking back to the first BTS concert I was able to attend in person by a sheer stroke of luck, I remember the feeling of loneliness fondly. Getting a concert ticket for one. Buying a plane ticket for one. The sea of purple at the gate and on the plane. Feeling in the wrong because I was able to identify ARMY around me, but was ARMY able to identify me? I'm not so sure. Getting dropped off at the concert venue alone and watching the pairs and groups of ARMY navigate merch lines, food truck lines together. Taking photos or handing out gifts they spent time making for ARMY. Singing and dancing together. There was ARMY everywhere I looked, and yet I was alone.

I stood in a merch line alone knowing the only sweatshirt and bandana I was remotely interested in spending money on were already sold out, and so I bought one of the only things left, a shirt that wasn't even for the concert I was attending, just to have some proof of my existence. If nothing, there will be a credit card transaction that exists in my name and I can say that I spoke to someone, even if it was just a staff member pretending not to notice me stumble over my words and push down the tears that welled up when they asked me if that was all I wanted. It wasn't, but I nodded and said thank you.

I found my gate alone and confirmed I was in the right spot with another staff member, who glanced at my ticket and pointed to where a line was already forming three hours before we were even scheduled to be let in. I waited in line at my gate alone. I managed to start up a short conversation with someone in front of me. They asked if I flew in for the concert, and I said yes. Their brows rose and a look of concern flooded their eyes, they asked, "Alone?" I said yes.

I got into the venue alone and found my seat alone. And I sat down, alone. I stood amongst a sold out stadium and yet for the entire duration of the concert, I was alone. I found the courage to ask someone next to me to take a photo for me. They took two and they were kind of blurry and I didn't like how I looked in them, but I said thank you and smiled behind my mask. I watched as they returned to their friend, both of them wearing coordinated outfits, and they asked me to take a photo for them. I took three with flash and three without flash and let them look at them in between to decide what they liked and didn't like and whether they wanted to change poses or have the background be the stage or the stadium. And then I took three more. When they were satisfied they thanked me and then I sat back down. Alone.

When the show started and BTS appeared on stage, I was happy even though I was alone. I was so fascinated by everything that was happening, but the one thing I can never unsee is the endless rows of ARMY and their glowing light sticks. The lights flashed and changed colours and at one point the crowd unknowingly spelled out "I ♡ ARMY" and I couldn't have agreed more. I cannot explain to you how many crucial live moments I missed on stage at this concert while I stood simply mesmerised by the presence of ARMY. For a fleeting moment I believed I was a part of it all, and yet I was alone.

When the concert ended, I left alone. That night I laid in bed alone, every time I shut my eyes all I saw was the endless floating, glowing orbs. Eventually I drifted off to sleep, tired, happy, and so very alone.

It feels wrong to remember the concert like this. It feels inadequate to write these feelings out at the same time as cold tears roll down my face and come to meet at the base of my chin. I am afraid to be honest about these feelings because I am worried that admitting to the feeling of loneliness in those moments (and even now) will negate the feeling of happiness and *Euphoria* that I also experienced. As if it isn't possible for us to experience polar opposite emotions at once. As if it isn't human to have emotions we can't always properly define. What better way to round out a critique on dualities and fighting the binary when I am barely capable of justifying my own polarising emotions. I keep telling myself that although it feels wrong to remember the concert this way, that doesn't change the fact that this is exactly how I felt. I do not hesitate to venture that this is possibly how others may have felt as well.

ARMY is many things but as we've come to learn, ARMY is hurting.[3] Therefore, I feel as though it is safe to say that my loneliness is not something I am experiencing alone. My loneliness, although unique to me, is shared. Just as I believe my queerness is. My transness. Even my journey of loving myself more and more each day. All of these things and more are mine and mine *alone*, while simultaneously being experienced and lived by so many others in so many different ways. ARMY and non-ARMY alike. I won't overcome my loneliness any quicker than I will overcome a system of power such as the idol and fan binary, or even begin to sense some version of progress within my gender journey, but it took me until very recently to realise that overcoming these situations and feelings should not be the ultimate goal. No one knows what the outcome will be, but the process and the journey we take to get there is what we will remember even if no one else does. I remember finding BTS. I remember my ongoing journey with my gender identity. I remember the feeling of learning to love myself again and again. And I remember ARMY.

> "*If I had taken courage and stood in front of you, would everything have been different now*"
>
> –*The Truth Untold*, BTS[1]

To ARMY

My name is Ran. I am ARMY. This is my story.

References

[1] BTS. (2018). The truth untold [Song]. On *Love yourself: Answer*. Big Hit Entertainment; Doolset. (2018). *The truth untold* [Translation].

[2] Harris, B., & Raatz, S. (2021). *Music spotlight presents BTS the ultimate activity fanbook*. Centennial Spotlight.

[3] Eaglehawk, W. (2020). *Idol limerence: The art of loving bts as phenomena*. Revolutionaries.

[4] Lancaster, R. N., & Leonardo, D. M. (1997). *The gender/sexuality reader: Culture, history, political economy*. Routledge.

[5] Stryker, S. (2006). (De)Subjugated knowledges: An introduction to transgender studies. In *The transgender studies reader*. Routledge.

[6] Halberstam, J. (2018) *Trans*: A quick and quirky account of gender variability*. University of California Press.

[7] Simien, J. (2017, April 28). Dear white people "Chapter II". *Dear white people*. [Episode] Netflix.

[8] Henderson, O. (2017, April 28). *Dear white people recap: Finding your label.* Vulture.

CPSIA information can be obtained
at www.ICGtesting.com
Printed in the USA
JSHW030315100323
38730JS00002B/159

9 780645 339260